Du

brilliant

freelancer

freelancer

Discover the power of your own success

Leif Kendall

Prentice Hall
is an imprint of

Harlow, England • London • New York • Boston • San Francisco • Toronto • Sydney • Singapore • Hong Kong
Tokyo • Seoul • Taipei • New Delhi • Cape Town • Madrid • Mexico City • Amsterdam • Munich • Paris • Milan

PEARSON EDUCATION LIMITED

Edinburgh Gate
Harlow CM20 2JE
Tel: +44 (0)1279 623623
Fax: +44 (0)1279 431059
Website: www.pearsoned.co.uk

First published in Great Britain in 2011

© Pearson Education 2011

The right of Leif Kendall to be identified as author of this work has been
asserted by him in accordance with the Copyright, Designs and Patents Act
1988.

Pearson Education is not responsible for the content of third party internet
sites.

ISBN: 978-0-273-74463-4

British Library Cataloguing-in-Publication Data
A catalogue record for this book is available from the British Library

Library of Congress Cataloging-in-Publication Data
Kendall, Leif.
   Brilliant freelancer : discover the power of your own success /
Leif Kendall. – 1st ed.
      p. cm.
   Includes index.
   ISBN 978-0-273-74463-4 (pbk.)
   1. Self-employed–Handbooks, manuals, etc. I. Title.
   HD8036.K46 2011
   650.1–dc22

                                                                2011002681

10 9 8 7 6 5 4 3 2 1
15 14 13 12 11

Typeset in 10/14pt Plantin Regular by 3
Printed in Great Britain by Henry Ling Ltd, at the Dorset Press, Dorchester,
Dorset

To Megan, for encouraging me to do the right thing.

Contents

About the author

Leif Kendall is a freelance web content writer and a passionate advocate of the freelance way of life. He began freelancing in 2008 after more than a decade in jobs that weren't quite right. Going freelance was a gamble that paid off.

Leif is now a well-established freelance writer, helping a wide variety of clients express themselves clearly. He also organises WriteClub, an informal networking group for all kinds of writers. When he's not writing stuff for clients he looks after his son, hangs out with his wife, cooks spicy food and rides bikes.

Acknowledgements

I owe a big thanks – thanks for helping me write this book and thanks for helping me be a freelancer – to lots of people, including Ellen De Vries, Premasagar Rose, Michael Bailey, Paul Silver, Matt Pearson, Anna Bertmark, Natasha Stuart, Evie Milo, Simon Booth-Lucking, Alex Cowell, Maxine Sheppard, Darren Fell, Will McInnes, Rosie Sherry, James McCarthy, Jacky Misson, Tim Misson, the members of the Brighton Farm freelancers group, John Williams and Samantha Jackson. Thanks also to my family, especially Joan Kendall and Sophie Earl, for their generous assistance with childcare. To my son Asher and my wife Megan: thanks for being patient while I wrote this book.

Our freelance friends

This book includes the ideas of a few talented freelancers that I interviewed before writing a word.

- Paul Silver – freelance PHP programmer and organiser of the Brighton Farm.
  www.paulsilver.co.uk
  www.brightonfarm.com
- Anna Bertmark – freelance sound technician.
  http://atticsound.net

- Matt Pearson – freelance Flash programmer, digital artist and author.

  http://zenbullets.com/blog

- Natasha Stuart – freelance writer, personal trainer and model.

  www.missmatahari.com

- Simon Booth-Lucking – freelance digital producer.

  www.boothlucking.co.uk

- Evie Milo – freelance web designer and digital agency owner.

  www.my-igloo.net

Publisher's acknowledgements

The publisher is grateful to the following for permission to reproduce copyright material:

Jo Cheung for the screenshot from **http://saintbarbie. wordpress.com** reproduced on page 38; Lorraine Jardim for the screenshot from **www.elliejphotography.co.uk** reproduced on page 38; Sara Duane-Gladden for the screenshot from **http:// sites.google.com/site/snduane** reproduced on page 39; and Evie Milo of Eskymo New Media Design for the contract template from **www.eskymo.co.uk** reproduced on pages 231–2.

In some instances we have been unable to trace the owners of copyright material, and we would appreciate any information that would enable us to do so.

Foreword

My first freelance contract was hard won. I'd spent several months getting the hang of this new world of finding projects and selling myself. Finally I landed something I loved in a very cool internet startup. They offered me a full-time job but I managed to turn it into a three-day-week contract paying me the same amount.

I was hooked.

Since that point more than 12 years ago, freelancing has led me into all sorts of interesting places and projects. I've worked with award-winning startups, global corporations and household names. I've worked on projects in Europe and Africa, written a piece of software that ended up in London's Science Museum, changed career completely, started my own company, and finally become a bestselling author with *Screw Work, Let's Play: How to do what you love and get paid for it*. Try doing all that in a conventional job!

One of the great pleasures of freelancing is that you are finally in charge of your own career – and that means you can take it wherever you want to go.

Brilliant Freelancer will help you get started quickly and easily. Leif manages to do what no one else has done – give the practical information you need to get started as a freelancer while making it simple and, above all, fun. (This has got to be the first book on freelancing that actually made me laugh out loud.)

Because really that's the point of being a successful freelancer – it's just a lot more interesting, exciting and fun than being stuck in a job. Even if it's sometimes a real challenge too.

Fortunately Leif eases some of those challenges – how to earn your first gig, what to do if you run out of money, deciding whether you need a limited company, setting your rate, haggling on price, and managing clients to keep both of you happy.

Whether you're considering taking that first leap from a job or you're already freelancing and ready to move up a gear, read *Brilliant Freelancer* and make a start today.

John Williams
Author of Screw Work, Let's Play: How to do what you love and get paid for it *(Prentice Hall, 2010)*

Introduction

Whatever you can do or dream you can, begin it. Boldness has genius, power and magic in it.   Johann Wolfgang von Goethe

Whether you're new to freelancing or a seasoned freelance operative, you've come to the right place. This book is about being a *brilliant* freelancer. It's about working smarter so you can enjoy a happy, productive and profitable freelance life. It's about building a long-term freelance career. And it's about your next steps – directions you might take if your ambitions become too big for freelancing.

Freelancing is a *challenging* way to make a living. It may bring you more freedom, but it will probably bring you more responsibility too. You may love working from home, but will you also love the irregular pay cheques, or the demanding clients? We'll look at freelancing from every angle, considering the challenges just as much as the fun stuff.

Great freelancers are made, not born. You become adept at freelancing by doing just that – *freelancing*. No freelancer is ever perfect when they start. Freelancers learn through hard work and hard knocks. Failure is edifying. And you'll never fail if you never do anything at all.

Oh, and you're scared, right? That's natural – I don't know many freelancers that didn't have doubts at the start. It's hard to quit a job when you haven't got another one to replace it. If you're moving into freelancing after a spell of unemployment, you may feel you have less to lose, but remain apprehensive about the new challenges you will face. Well, you're not alone. Only the fool-hardy or the careless would jump into something as significant as freelancing without the tickle of butterflies in the belly. As you stand on the precipice, remember that going freelance is a major life choice but it is not permanent. If you and freelancing don't get along, you can always return to regular employment.

If you're worried about making such a big change, my own experiences may reassure you: I quit my job when my son was three months old and I was the main breadwinner. I had very little experience, a couple of clients, no qualifications, a lot of trepidation and hardly any savings. I didn't go to university and my career trajectory was, well, let's not even go there. In spite of these factors I've hammered out a successful and liberating freelance career and can scarcely imagine taking a salary ever again. By leaving the cloister of company life I've discovered all kinds of latent talents. Freelancing has changed my world – not least because Sundays no longer herald that ominous dread of Monday and the return to work. Mondays still mean the return to work, but now it's my work, and I'm the boss.

PART 1

The freelance essentials: what you need to know before you take the leap

The journey of a million miles begins with a single step.

Chinese proverb

You are starting something big. This is the beginning of a great adventure, so you may feel terrified just as much as you feel excited. And because becoming a freelancer is a multi-faceted challenge, packed with tasks, goals and decisions, you can easily feel overwhelmed with stuff to do, your mind a whirring whirligig of ideas and fears. But don't panic. Freelancing is tough, but enjoyable, and you're going to enjoy it. Trust me.

There are all kinds of choices for you to make, but most can wait. So while the early parts of this book deal with the mechanics of getting started, feel free to skip ahead to the stuff that's important to you now. Maybe you urgently need to find work, or maybe you need a smarter approach to client management, or maybe you're wondering how to avoid loneliness if you're working alone – if any of these apply to you then you can probably worry about your VAT status later. When you've addressed the pressing issues, come back here. But if you're not in a hurry, let's start at the beginning.

CHAPTER 1

What does it mean to be a freelancer?

The word 'freelance' harks back to a time when noble knights slaughtered beasties and rescued damsels. Carrying *lances*, they were *free* to work with anyone that needed their armour-clad services. Nowadays we've dropped the swords and sorcery and deal exclusively with businesses, public sector groups, NGOs and charities, both large and small.

brilliant definitions

Freelancer
A self-employed person who sells their professional services by the hour, day or project.

Contractor
A self-employed person who sells their professional services for contracted periods of times (anything from a few weeks to many months).

To understand the freelance landscape, think about it from the perspective of the business that hires you. Businesses need all kinds of skills, services and products in order to trade. Specialist skills may be needed rarely, but when the need arises, they need experts rather than generalists. Rather than hire all kinds of staff with skills they only need once a year, they hire freelancers. So once a year (or whenever) they can pick up the phone and know that an experienced professional will be available to do their important work.

The experienced professional at the end of the phone is *you*. So while the etymology of the word freelance really doesn't matter, it's given us an excuse to reflect on the *value* that freelancers offer. And value is critical to the life of a freelancer, because value is what you're selling, value is what your clients are buying and value will be central to your marketing.

? brilliant questions

Q Is now a good time to go freelance?

A Depending on who you ask, it's always the right time to go freelance, or never the right time to go freelance. There will always be work for freelancers, but as the economy rises and dips (or disintegrates), opportunities for freelancers shift and shuffle. Also, every profession and industry varies – so while journalists might be struggling to find work, plumbers might be inundated with work. To get a realistic view of your chances of success, speak to other freelancers to find out how they're faring.

Q We're in the middle of a recession, so is it madness to go freelance now?

A During a recession, many companies are forced to reduce their full-time staff. Ergo, they may need freelancers to fill the gaps when a need arises. However, some businesses do the opposite – using lots of freelancers during the good times and then bringing the talent in-house when times are bad, because a permanent crew may be cheaper. So there's no simple answer to whether you will be safe as a freelancer in a recession.

Q Do I have what it takes to go freelance?

A Yes, you do, because all you need now is a desire to succeed and a willingness to *try*. You may feel unsure that you have what it takes, but remember that freelancers become capable by being freelancers. So don't expect to have all the skills you need before you start. The worst-case scenario is that you enjoy freelancing but can't find enough work to cover your bills. In which case, you may need to start searching for a full-time or part-time job.

Contractors are freelancers too

Contractors are another kind of freelancer, who seek work that tends to last longer than freelance gigs. For example, a software company may hire a few programmers on six-month contracts to build a specific application. Once the six months is up the contractors are let loose and they set about looking for another contract.

There is no clear dividing line between contractors and free-lancers; some freelancers do contracting, and some contractors do freelancing. Contracting tends to pay well, but contractors are more likely to spend time in their client's office and lose some of the freedom that freelancers cherish. Freelancing gives you freedom, but it comes loaded with insecurity. You can begin as a freelancer and become a contractor, or vice versa.

> freelancing gives you freedom

Why do people go freelance?

This is the perfect time to hear from our freelance friends:

 'I wanted to determine my own career – to follow the technologies I thought were most promising. I couldn't get that freedom from a job – the only way was to go it alone.'

Matt Pearson

'I was ready for a new direction in life. I'd been very successful within a business but when we reached a crossroads it felt like the right time to follow that new direction.'

Simon Booth-Lucking

'I wanted to explore the wider industry that I work in, instead of being cocooned within a company.'

Anna Bertmark

'I've never been anything other than freelance. My dad was self-employed so I always knew that regular employment was not my only option.'

Natasha Stuart

'I was made redundant and I'd had a taste for freelancing because lots of my friends were freelance. It felt like the right time.'

Paul Silver

How do you become a freelancer?

Technically, quitting your job is all it takes to become a freelancer. But freelancers are defined by their work and their clients, so the real way you become a freelancer is by establishing a base of clients and a portfolio of work. The game of finding work will consume much of your time and mental energy – especially when work is scarce and times are tough.

If you decide to go freelance and earn your own income, you'll need to notify HM Revenue and Customs (HMRC). You can register as self-employed online at the HMRC website.

Notifying HMRC is all you really need to do to become freelance. You can live without an accountant (for now), book-keeping software (just use a spreadsheet), an office (use

> notifying HMRC is all you really need to do to become freelance

your home, cafés, libraries, or anywhere you can find a comfortable space) or any of the million things freelancers use to make their lives easier (and more complicated).

So for now, let's assume you're ready to go.

 brilliant recap

- As a freelancer you offer value to your clients by giving them pay-as-you-go expertise.

- Contractors and freelancers are both self-employed but contractors tend to work on longer jobs.

- You must notify HMRC that you're becoming self-employed.

- The challenge of becoming freelance is finding clients – so don't get distracted by the accessories of freelancing.

CHAPTER 2

Are you ready for freelancing?

You ou may be tempted by the freelance lifestyle, but unsure if you have what it takes to succeed. That's natural, and the truth is there's really no way to know whether you'll take to freelancing. Until you try, you'll never know.

Some books about freelancing offer tests to check if you have the skills to succeed; you answer questions about your contacts, skills, confidence and training, and hope your score is above the minimum level someone decided makes some semblance of sense. But frankly, it's all poppycock.

That kind of test is nonsense because it's *okay* if you aren't perfect at pitching ideas to clients. It's fine if your knees turn to jelly when you think about networking events. It's fine if you never went to university and it's definitely fine that you don't have a fat network of powerful connections. It's fine to start freelancing without these things because you may never need them, and if you do need them you can seek them out. So we won't be doing any tests.

However, it *is* worth reflecting on your motivations for becoming a freelancer, because your motivations are what will keep you pushing relentlessly forward, day after day, even in the face of rejection, failure and frustration.

 action

Why do you want to be a freelancer?

Think about what draws you towards freelancing, and make a list of your motivations.

Compare your own motivations with the lists of good and bad motivations below. Hopefully most of your motivations will fall into the 'good' category. If you are motivated by bad things (or pure evil) then maybe a freelance career isn't right for you just now. But again, this isn't science. So if it feels right, just do it.

Good motivations

- You want to get more experience than you can get working with one company.
- You want to make your own choices and steer your own ship.
- You want more flexibility about where and when you work.
- You want to control the kind of work you do.
- You want to behave less like a pure technician and more like a business.

Bad motivations

- You want to work less hard.
- You hate people.
- You heard you might earn £300 per day.
- You struggle to get out of bed for your day job.

Freelancing vs permanent employment

Is freelancing really for you? Or are the perks of regular employment too good to refuse? Let's look at the pros and cons of freelancing over permanent employment.

The advantages of freelancing

- You get to work wherever you want.
- You can focus on the work you enjoy.
- You can potentially earn a better income.
- You can learn more and assume more responsibility.
- Work can be more flexible to accommodate your family's needs.
- You'll always know exactly how rosy or bleak your future is.
- You can change your colleagues if you don't like the current batch.

The advantages of permanent employment

- You get paid every month.
- You have an annual holiday entitlement.
- You get paid even when you're ill.
- If you cruise along on autopilot, you *might* still get paid.
- If your employer is stable and successful then your job is secure.
- You always have colleagues.
- You may get paid to train.

Why freelancers are just very small businesses

Your freelance career can take all kinds of directions. You may get lucky and find a few large clients who offer you retainers, or you may have skills that are so desperately needed that work always finds you. Or you may have to fight hard for every job, investing lots of time in marketing. However your career unfolds, you will have to deal with more than just the challenges of finding and completing work. Because even though freelancers are fleet-footed independent operatives, they still have administration to take care of, accounts to file, invoices to raise, clients to call, equipment to maintain and late-payers to chase – basically all the functions of a normal business, but on a smaller scale.

Think of yourself as a small business, because that's what you are. If you ever struggle as a freelancer, ask what a business would do in your situation. You'll probably find that the solution to your problem can be found by adopting business tactics. Don't be afraid of picking up business books for ideas. The only difference between you and a small business is that *you* are the only product.

don't be afraid of picking up business books for ideas

As a small business, you'll be in sole charge of absolutely everything. You'll be manager, director, salesperson, book-keeper, administrator, project manager, account handler, technician, IT support and the cleaner. Go freelance and you will soon find yourself exploring business areas beyond your usual remit. That's great if you're curious and versatile, but if you just want to practise your trade or hone your skills, you may get frustrated with freelancing's wide-ranging demands on your time.

 **brilliant** action

Research the market

One simple way to reduce your anxiety about leaping into freelancing is to learn about the market you're entering. By chatting to other freelancers you can assess the amount of work available and your chances of success. Try to answer these questions:

● How busy are other freelancers in your sector?

● Are there any gaps in the market?

● Where are other freelancers finding work?

● Are other freelancers travelling out of town to get work?

brilliant recap

- There's no sure-fire way to know if you're ready to go freelance, but assess your motivations to make sure you're not driven by the dark side.

- You don't need to be a well-rounded freelancer before you start freelancing, because you'll gather skills as you go.

- Talk to other freelancers to gauge the marketplace.

- Freelancers are small, simple businesses.

- Look to traditional business advice for solutions to your challenges.

CHAPTER 3

Make a smooth transition into freelancing

One of the wonderful things about freelancing is that you can start today. You can begin freelancing with no investment, no planning, no cost and very little risk.

Freelance lite

If you have a full-time job that gets in the way of being a freelancer, start *moonlighting*. Moonlighting means to work in the hours you're not busy with your day job. By being cunning with your use of time, you can dabble with freelancing without risking anything. As John Williams writes in *Screw Work, Let's Play*, 'you no longer have to mortgage your house to start something. You can go online and get started in an afternoon – for free.' You can test the waters and get a taste for how easy or difficult freelancing might be for you, and you can do it all today.

> you can dabble with freelancing without risking anything

Part-time job, part-time freelance

There are infinite ways to begin your freelance career. If you're feeling nervous about leaping from regular employment into freelancing, why not get a part-time job and use your free time to dabble in freelancing? You'll have enough time to build your freelance career but enough guaranteed income to reduce your money worries. Given the current job market, it's natural to be hesitant about leaving a comfortable job, so blending a permanent position with freelance work is a great way to get started.

It's impossible to say exactly how you should get started because every new freelancer has different skills and experiences. You may be brand new to your field or you may be a well-known professional with a bulging portfolio – and the challenges for each are different.

Starting with nothing

You have no experience and no clients, and your freelance adventures are entirely ahead of you. If you feel uneasy about charging clients for services you haven't delivered before, volunteer your time. There will always be businesses that need your help, and if you can help them for free they'll be thrilled. But don't spend too much time working for nothing. Remember: you're just testing the waters here. So if you do two or three pieces of work on a volunteer basis and they go well, you should start charging.

brilliant tip

Working for free is a dangerous tactic – so use it wisely. It's fine to work for free occasionally, as long as your loss is balanced by a gain. If your loss of time is balanced by a benefit to your portfolio or a chance to try a new skill or discipline, then it's okay.

Starting with something

If you're an experienced professional then your transition into freelancing could be easy. You'll still have to work hard to find jobs – but at least your portfolio and reputation are already established.

What challenges might you face? Beware complacency. You're great at doing the work, but are you great at *finding* work? Are you great at selling? Can you find leads, pitch successfully and keep clients happy throughout difficult or challenging projects? Be confident in your skills, but remember that freelancing may bring new challenges for you to embrace.

Save cash before you quit your job

Before you quit your job, try to build up your savings. Remember that once your final pay cheque has landed, you're on your own. While you're busy getting your freelance career off the ground you still need to pay your bills. Conventional wisdom suggests you should save the equivalent of three months' salary before you quit your job. If you can save that much money, please do. I managed to save one and a half months' salary before I became impatient and quit my job. So don't let the three-months' salary thing stand in your way, but do recognise that less money means less

> fear is a great motivator

security. Being less secure is not automatically a bad thing, because fear is a great motivator. If you have three months' worth of savings in the bank, will you feel forced to try every possible tactic to kick-start your freelance career, or will you drift along, only panicking (and acting) when you enter the third month? Where are you on the sliding scale of fear vs. motivation?

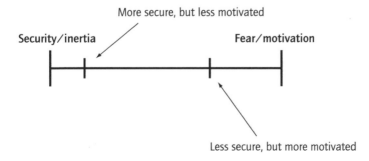

Reduce the figure you need to save by calculating your emergency survival budget. Include all your essential expenses and exclude luxuries. If you're worried about making a slow start to freelancing (and not having much cash), strip back all unnecessary costs. So fripperies like your gym membership, web-movie-download thing, organic vegetable box, cranial osteopathy treatment, weekly curry and personal trainer can all be put on hold. Pare back what you don't need until the trickle of work becomes a river full of fish made of cash.

Leap straight into freelancing

Bursting to go freelance, but struggling to prepare yourself? Perhaps you haven't got the time for moonlighting or you can't push yourself to call potential clients. For whatever reason, you're the kind of person that can't *be* freelance until you *go* freelance. Until you've left your job, you'll never be free to freelance. Paul Silver, organiser of Brighton's Farm freelancer group, was in the same boat: 'It wasn't going to happen until I was a freelancer,' he said – fully aware that the only way he could succeed as a freelancer was to leap right in.

> until you've left your job, you'll never be free to freelance

Maybe *your* way is to leap right in, without worrying too much about plans. That's absolutely fine and just because you haven't obsessively laid out your freelance future, you're no less likely to succeed. Indeed, your lack of planning may drive you onwards and push you to work harder and more persistently – because you have little to fall back on.

As Matt Pearson puts it: 'When you try freelancing, you have to accept that you might fail. You have to have the balls to give it a go.'

 **action**

Calculate your survival budget

Add up all your essential expenses – the things you can't possibly avoid – like:

- rent or mortgage payments
- electricity and gas
- water
- council tax
- food and household essentials
- telephone and broadband
- childcare costs
- car costs (tax, insurance, fuel, repayments)
- debt repayments (credit cards, loans, student loans)
- pension.

If you're in a relationship, make sure you factor in your partner's income and expenses too. And remember that this isn't a traditional budget – you're including only the costs you can't live without. Add your essential costs together. The total amount is your survival budget. As a freelancer, the money you earn is not all yours; account for tax by adding 20–25 per cent to your costs. Now you have your break-even value.

If you consistently earn less than your break-even value then you need to try something different (e.g. bolder marketing), consider a mix of permanent or temporary part-time work and freelancing, or return to full-time employment and come back to freelancing another time.

Compare your survival budget with your savings – how many months could you survive on basic rations with the cash you have?

Divide your survival budget by your hourly rate to see how many hours you'll need to work each month to break even. Do the same with your day rate.

What if I run out of money?

First, don't panic. You *can* earn money in the short-term and continue with your long-term freelance plans. Short-term quick-fixes that can generate cash include:

- contracting
- cash-in-hand work
- part-time work
- temping.

 'In the early days of my freelance career, when work was scarce, I accepted a short-term contract that was many miles from home. I stayed in the cheapest B&B I could find. It wasn't ideal, but that project kept me going.'

Paul Silver

While temping or part-time work can be a good short-term earner, remember that both pay a fraction of your freelance rates – so before you seek these quick-fixes, call every potential client you can think of. It's infinitely better to spend time marketing than it is to get diverted by temporary solutions.

Don't wait to get paid

In the early days, you need to get paid quickly. So tell your clients that your payment terms are seven days from the invoice date, and you'll be invoicing the moment your work is done. Better yet, request a 50 per cent deposit, with the balance payable within seven days. And make sure you chase payments mercilessly, as though your life depends on it. If your cash flow is really tight, call clients the day before your invoices are due and check that your invoice is due to be paid on time. Many small businesses will be able to accept short payment terms, but larger companies will have preset payment terms that they cannot deviate from – often 30+ days after the invoice date – so accept that not every client will pay you according to your terms. For more on credit control see Chapter 21.

> not every client will pay you according to your terms

Freelancing with a family – and persuading the doubters

Going freelance is a scary choice for anyone to make. But if you have your own family then going freelance is even scarier. Is it fair to risk your family's security? The short answer: *hell yes*. The long answer: well, security is relative. A permanent job might feel secure, but in reality there's nothing to guarantee that your boss isn't running the company into the ground. By the time you realise things are bad, it's too late. So your apparently secure job dissolves in a puff of smoke. As a freelancer, you will be intimately acquainted with the risks you face. You'll also be free to respond to risks and take action when required. Even if you run your own business into the ground, at least you'll have advance warning.

But clearly this all depends on your own capabilities and your own preferences. You may prefer to be part of a larger organisation, pulling together towards a shared goal. Or you may prefer to flex your own talents and seek the limits of your potential, under your own command.

If you're contemplating going freelance, you may encounter resistance from within your family. People close to you may worry that your plans are risky and unsettling. To most people, jobs represent security, so they may think you mad for voluntarily leaving a paying job. Try to enlighten the doubters, but friends and family who worry about your financial security may remain permanently concerned, even after you've proven that you can make freelancing work.

The impact of freelancing on family life

Is freelancing a good or bad option for mums and dads? Well, it's a bit of both. Being freelance gives you the potential for more freedom, but what freelancing gives you with one hand it takes away with the other. So freelancing gives you flexibility, but it also gives you more work.

In *theory* you can take time off whenever you like, but in *reality* you have to get jobs done, and you have all kinds of admin and marketing to do too. Freelancing is the job that keeps on giving. And you'll definitely feel less stressed if you leave a job that makes you unhappy, but at the same time you have a whole new batch of worries, like worrying about getting enough work, or worrying about getting paid. Going freelance just swaps one kind of worry for another kind of worry. Will you prefer the stress of freelancing or the stress of your day job? That's for you to discover.

> freelancing is the job that keeps on giving

Some days, when work has been scarce, my wife has noticed a gloom descend over my mood – a gloom that I cannot hide. And when my freelance career was little more than a fragile baby bird, my wife had to live with a man who was not really there – my mind racing with plans and schemes, running over my prospects, finances and my chances of survival. Luckily, this stage doesn't last long. After a few months things settle down, and you'll be able to forget about work for minutes at a time! But seriously, freelancing is not a way to work for people who don't want to work, or for people who don't want to *think* about their work, because freelancing demands brain space.

What if I hate freelancing?

Freelancing is a delightful way to work, but it's not right for everyone. You may try freelancing and dislike it, or you may love it but struggle to find enough work – or you may discover that you need to be managed to work well. Whatever the case, there's a chance that freelancing just isn't right for you.

You may feel despondent, or depressed, or just worried about finding a job that pays. Don't worry. If at any point you feel concerned about your prospects, seek out other freelancers and ask their advice – simply email or call freelancers you find via Google or attend networking events (see Chapter 8 for more on networking). And remember that even if freelancing is not for you, or the time isn't quite right – then at least you had the courage to try something bold, rather than live life wondering.

 **recap**

- You can build up experience by working for free.
- Start freelancing before you leave your job – make use of every spare minute.
- Make sure you get paid quickly.
- Calculate your survival budget so you know exactly how much you need to earn each month.
- You may feel it's impossible to get started while you're employed – so maybe you need to quit your job before you can get anywhere.
- Freelancing isn't right for everyone and there's nothing wrong with returning to regular employment.

CHAPTER 4

Your first freelance jobs: how to find them and how to quote for them

For many freelancers, the hunt for jobs is a big part of their life. Work may be plentiful, but so too are freelancers. Getting in front of clients and piercing their consciousness requires a persistent effort. Few freelancers find jobs effortlessly. After a few years on the scene you may be able to rely on referrals and repeat business, but until then the search for work can be an arduous battle.

Finding your first clients

We'll look at marketing in more detail in Part 2 – for now you just need to get the word out that you're a freelancer and you're available. Tell people: 'I'm starting out as a freelance tree surgeon and I'm offering a few free projects to build my portfolio. So if you know anyone who needs help with a hedge, give me a shout.'

Now you've decided to try freelancing, you need to talk about it, lots. Tell your friends and family. Tell the people you meet. Look for opportunities. Become mildly self-centred and whenever anyone talks to you about a problem they have, consider if your services could solve it. Develop a one-track mind. Potential clients are all around you. Filter conversations through the muslin of your freelance career. Never be pushy, rude or obnoxious, but look for opportunities to help others.

develop a one-track mind

Develop your online presence

The web is your friend and it can do miraculous things – bringing you jobs, friends and fame down the wires. Ultimately, you will need a website. If you don't have the time, money or skills to build a website you can make use of free website builders or social media websites to develop your presence online.

Why bother going online? Because most recruitment begins with Google. When a potential client considers using you, they'll Google you. If they find nothing, they know nothing. Disappointed and unfulfilled, they'll swiftly move on to your competitors, who will inevitably have rich online presences. And you, Mr or Ms Invisible, are already forgotten.

> most recruitment begins with Google

Before you build your web presence, follow Paul Silver's advice and 'Google yourself'. What can you find? There may be traces of former lives – naked pictures, drunken revelries or obnoxious opinion. If possible, prune away the embarrassing words and images. Your online identity should be manicured and curated – crafted to represent your current professional self.

Now you can concentrate on building a digital presence. Your main objectives are to show people:

- who you are
- what you do
- what you've done (your experience or portfolio)
- who you know
- what you want (what kinds of work or opportunity they should approach you with)

- how you work (your processes, what clients can expect from working with you)
- how to contact you
  - your phone number
  - email address
  - postal address.

Use social media to create a fast, free web presence

There are many excellent ways to get your name online for free, including:

- LinkedIn
- Behance.net (for creatives who want to show off their portfolio)
- Twitter
- Facebook.

Use easy website creators

You can build a website today, without any web design knowledge and without spending a penny. Your website can go forth into the unknown, returning with a bounty of hot prospects, lush clients and gilded opportunities. While good websites require hard work and perseverance to get right, they return your efforts many times over. See Chapter 9 for a fuller view of web marketing.

Here are three websites created with free or low-cost tools:

WordPress.com – **http://saintbarbie.wordpress.com**

Create.net – **www.elliejphotography.co.uk**

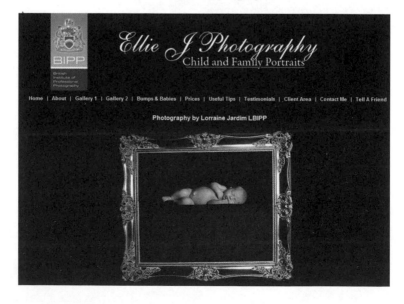

Google Sites – **http://sites.google.com/site/snduane**

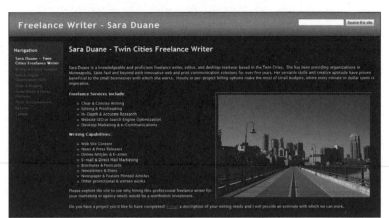

WordPress, Create and Google Sites are all designed for people with no technical knowledge. So even if you're a technophobe, you *should* be able to create something online. And if you get stuck, you'll find plenty of help in online forums, help centres and FAQs.

My own website building experience

My own site grew out of a free WordPress website. So my first domain was something like **www.kendallcopywriting. wordpress.com**. I eventually met two kind web developers, and in exchange for a curry they moved my website on to my own domain (**www.kendallcopywriting.co.uk**). To achieve this I simply had to buy a domain (I used **www.godaddy.com**) and pay for web hosting (I used **www.purplecloud.com**).

So I started with a very basic website that was crafted out of favours, open source software (WordPress) and a healthy dose of experimentation (I regularly broke bits of code). My original website was shabby, but it was *functional*. It allowed me to offer my services to the world and start blogging. My amateur website, which cost less than £100, brought me thousands of pound's worth of jobs. Without the help of my website I'm not sure I would have survived my first year of freelancing. As soon as I could afford to pay for web designers and developers to enhance my website, I did. Even then, the progress and changes have been incremental and progressive – fixing small bugs and adding features gradually, as my budget allows.

Get out and meet people

Whoever you are and wherever you're going, you need to know *people*. There's a popular adage that 'people buy from people' which hints at the personal relationships behind many business deals. While ostensibly most business-to-business (B2B) deals are trades between two impersonal corporations, they are in fact bargains conducted by people, between people. As a freelancer you're going to be selling yourself to other people, so you need to know plenty of people.

Networking is often the difference between freelancers who flourish and those who fail. Good networking isn't about circling a room full of suits, delivering a polished elevator pitch and swapping business cards. Good networking is about getting to know people and looking for ways to help them. We'll look at networking in more detail in Chapter 8, but for now you should start looking for interesting events in your area. Networking opportunities are often disguised as other things – so remember that chances to meet people and expand your circle of friends and acquaintances aren't always called 'networking'. Your football club, book group or fellow volunteers are all part of your network.

> good networking is about getting to know people

If you're nervous about networking, that's okay. *Everyone* gets nervous about networking until they try it. I delayed my first foray into networking for several weeks because I was worried about trying to sell myself to strangers. When I finally managed to push myself to try it, I was massively relieved; the group was friendly and very informal. So if you feel anxious at the thought of networking, I recommend you start with an informal event – something that's barely networking. Maybe take a friend with you so you don't have to walk through the door alone. Networking events are designed to bring people together, and many event organisers know just how scary networking can seem, so they work hard to make their events easy and inviting for new people. Most cities have their own networking groups, so search for meet-ups near you (just Google 'networking *mytown*' or use **www.meetup.com** to find groups).

Examples of networking associations include:

- your local chamber of commerce
- professional or trade associations
- likemind.us.

Introducing ... you!

Freelance audio technician Anna Bertmark used a novel approach to make connections when she started out. Rather than assault her ideal clients with bland emails, Anna *asked people for advice*. By changing the nature of her enquiry into something less commonplace than an appeal for work, Anna was able to arrange a series of meetings with the people she wanted to work with. By asking for advice, Anna appealed to her clients' generous natures and managed to start relationships with potential clients.

Go back to your roots – freelance for your former employer

Many freelancers begin their careers by working for their old employers. So when you quit your job, be nice! Make your exit smooth and professional, because your old boss could become your new client. Be honest with your employer about your reasons for leaving. Going freelance is a positive step, so make sure they understand that you're leaving to explore new opportunities, not because you dislike their company.

Decide what to charge

Putting a price tag on *you* is one of the hardest tasks freelancers face. Determined to value yourself fairly, but wary of inflating your own worth, you may find it hard to get the balance right. The key to choosing the right rate is to work out what other freelancers are charging in your area and to charge roughly the same. That's worth repeating: *charge roughly the same*. Don't be Discount Dave, working for half the going rate, because there's no need.

If you're a virgin freelancer, fresh out of the box, charge roughly the same as other freelancers in your area, but at the lower end of the pricing spectrum. If you're a mature freelancer with bags of experience, place your rates at the higher end of the spectrum. For most people, the answer to the 'what to charge' question is: ask others what they charge for similar services and *charge roughly the same.*

How do you find out what other freelancers are earning? You can either ask your peers, potential clients or agents. You can try calling or emailing freelancers, clients or agencies, or you can review jobs online to get a feel for the going rates.

Inflate your rate

Your rate should move with you – so as your experience and skills grow, so should your rate. You may feel nervous about raising your rates, but as long as you can justify the increase to your clients (and take the time to explain your reasons) they should accept the change. Most clients are motivated by value just as much as by cost so they'll continue working with you if they believe your rates match your value. Clients who prioritise cost above all else are rarely good clients – and do you really want a client who only likes you because you're cheap? So while raising your rates may put you beyond the reach of some clients, it may drop you into the lap of better ones – those who expect to pay top dollar for the best people.

> most clients are motivated by value just as much as by cost

Know when to raise your rates

Telltale signs that it's time to raise your rates include when:

- you're constantly loaded with work
- you offer more than your peers
- you've gained lots of experience since your last rate change
- all your competitors charge more
- nobody ever quibbles over your rates
- people say 'wow that's cheap' when they get your quote.

Variable rates

Every job that comes your way will have its own value. There will be jobs for great companies that you would sell a kidney to get, and there will be jobs so unpleasant, for clients so odious, that you would sooner eat your own nose than get involved. But even the nose-eating job may be attractive if the price is right.

This is why having a variable rate is a good idea. When a job offers rewards like priceless experience, or a foot-in-the-door with a great client, or just a warm sense of satisfaction, you may decide to lower your rates in order to get the work. And if a job leaves you cold, hike your rates; you'll either scare off the client or secure a price that makes the work tolerable.

How to quote

The joy of finding a new client is often quelled by the complexities of quoting. You can make quoting easier, and less of a surprise for your clients, by discussing a few key details in advance. Chat about:

- **Project scope** – how much work does their project involve?
- **Deliverables** – exactly what are they expecting to receive from you?
- **Budgets** – roughly how much money do they have?
- **Timescales** – when are they expecting the work to be finished?

Great quotes take time

Preparing quotes is time consuming. You need to fully understand your client's needs, and then you need to explain how you will meet their needs, and define the costs involved. Your clients will evaluate the quotes they receive on more than just cost. So winning the job isn't about submitting the lowest quote. Winning quotes provide a clear rationale for the costs included, an explanation of your processes, lists of assumptions, deadlines, targets and penalties. Clients appreciate clear quotes that make sense. So take your time and ask someone to review your quote – it should make sense to a layperson.

> clients appreciate clear quotes that make sense

Discuss budgets with your clients

Talking about money can be a delicate dance on a tightrope. Misguided clients believe that great deals are achieved by hoodwinking their opponent into a bargain that benefits them while destroying their supplier. In reality, good deals are equal exchanges that benefit both parties, and being secretive about budgets is totally pointless.

Why you should endeavour to learn your client's budget

Let's imagine that you're the client. You want a brand new website. You have £500 to spend, but there's no way in hell you're going to tell anyone this, mainly because you think secrecy is a winning strategy, rather like in a game of cards. You approach three different web designers and ask them to quote for making you a website. They all assess your needs, devise a strategy for meeting them and prepare a quote. The quotes come in at £1500, £1750 and £3000. None of them are suitable. You, realising that your secrecy has worked against you, return to the three web designers and declare your actual budget. Two of the web designers decline, saying your budget is too small for them, while the third web designer prepares a new quote, removing the time previously allowed for luxuries like user research and photography. In this example, the secretive client has wasted a great deal of three people's time. As a freelancer you will encounter many people who will happily waste your time. Because your time is your only product, and your only real source of income, you need to guard it like a jealous lover.

Never submit quotes that are doomed to fail – simply get a rough idea of your client's budget first. If your client is reticent, don't push them to reveal their budget, but offer them a ballpark cost. Say something like, 'I think your project will cost in the region of £2000', and see how they react. If they start hyperventilating then you know you need to rethink – but if they don't flinch and say 'That's fine' then you know that a quote in that region will meet their approval.

Assumptions and project scope

Your quote is a chance to iron out the details of your business deal, and it's also the first place you and your client will turn if the arrangement goes bad. So when you prepare a quote, ask yourself, 'If this job goes bad, is there anything in my quote that could be used against me – are there any ambiguous details?' List the assumptions that your quote makes: for example, that you assume your client is supplying the materials, or that you assume the client will be ready to begin by a certain date, or you assume that the client will only take two days to provide feedback at each stage.

Fixed prices or hourly rates

There are a number of different ways to quote:

- **Fixed price** – you agree to do a job for a fixed amount of money. Your invoice will match the agreed price, regardless of how much time the job takes.
- **Hourly or daily rate** – your client will ask you to work for a period of time and you complete as much work as possible in that time.
- **Estimated costs** – you and your client agree that the work should take between x and y hours, so your final invoice must be within those limits.
- **Rolling costs** – your client agrees to pay your hourly rate for as long as the work takes, although you probably agree a rough estimate beforehand.

brilliant dos and don'ts

To prepare the best possible quotes:

Do

✔ Ask your client lots of intelligent, open-ended questions.

✔ Listen carefully to your client.

✔ Try to understand your client's problems.

✔ Look for unspoken desires – the things your client wants to achieve but isn't talking about.

✔ Define objectives, deliverables and responsibilities in your quote so nothing is left to chance.

Don't

✘ Assume anything (e.g. that your client is supplying resources).

✘ Expose yourself to later disputes by being vague.

✘ Ignore things you don't understand – seek clarification before quoting.

✘ Pluck numbers out of the air – be prepared to justify your costs.

Working on a fixed price basis

Many of your clients will want fixed price quotes. Without a fixed price your clients will be unable to budget and they will be at your mercy, while you are free to work ponderously over their project and invoice for as much as you fancy. In many respects, fixed price quotes are fair for you *and* your clients.

When preparing a fixed price quote it's essential that you specify the quantity of work included in your price (e.g. 45 pages of web copy with 16 fully edited photographs). Calculate how long it will take you to complete one unit of their work and then multiply the time by the quantity of work. This method is helpful because it gives you a clear basis for arriving at a final sum. If your client questions the total cost quoted, you can simply take them back to your calculations. If you can help your client to see that it takes you x hours to perform y, then they're more likely to accept your quote.

Examples:

20 web page templates $\times$ 3 hours per page = 60 hours.

210 magazine pages laid out $\times$ 1.5 hour per page = 315 hours.

16 electrical outlets installed $\times$ 30 minutes per outlet = 8 hours.

Protect yourself with a buffer

Fixed prices often work out well, but you should always include an element of padding or buffer in your quote. For example, if you estimate that it takes 30 minutes to install an electrical outlet, but when you start work you discover it actually takes you 45 minutes, you may have to spend several hours working for free. So always assume that things take a bit longer than you think. If a client wants a fixed price for an unusual project, ask to work on a sample so that you can assess the work involved. By doing a test you can also get a sense of how easy or difficult the client will be to work with.

> always assume that things take a bit longer than you think

When fixed prices start to move

With a fixed price quote, the quantity of work must also be fixed. If the work changes because the client wants more units of work, or additional services, then the quote must be revised. Make sure that any additional services are agreed in advance, in writing.

Negotiating with recruitment agencies

If you dip into contracting, then instead of quoting for projects you'll be agreeing an hourly or daily rate for a fixed period of time. And often you'll be negotiating with recruitment agents rather than the end client. Before you get to this stage, arm yourself with an understanding of your real worth. Know your market!

During negotiations try to remain cool and don't sound too eager. Try to delay negotiating your rate until you've met the client. If you can impress the client then you'll be in a stronger bargaining position – because by now the agent wants to get the contract wrapped up and avoid re-advertising the position.

 **brilliant** tip

Resources for contractors:

● www.contractorcalculator.co.uk

● www.contracteye.co.uk/index.shtml

Start saving for your tax bill

When your clients pay your invoices, the money you receive is not entirely yours. At the end of the year you'll need to pay tax on your earnings, so get into the habit of saving 20–25 per cent of your earnings in preparation.

 **brilliant** recap

● 'People buy from people' – so get to know more people.

● Make sure you have a presence on the web – don't be Mr or Ms Invisible.

- Decide your standard rates but be prepared to adjust them when it benefits you.

- Try to learn your client's budget so you can submit a suitable proposal.

- Quotes take time to prepare – so don't rush a quote unless you don't want the job.

- Understand your market value before you negotiate contracts with an agent.

- Put aside 20–25 per cent of your income for tax.

CHAPTER 5

Becoming a company

W hen you become self-employed you'll need to choose a legal status. The two most popular options are *limited company* and *sole trader*. Both have their own benefits and drawbacks, so let's look at what they involve.

Sole trader

It's easy to become a sole trader. Simply notify HM Revenue and Customs that you are self-employed. Make sure you notify HMRC within three months of becoming self-employed or you risk a fine. If your income exceeds £70,000 (at the current threshold) then you'll also need to register for VAT. As a sole trader you'll need to complete an annual tax return. Many sole traders complete their own tax assessments online, eliminating the need for an accountant.

As a sole trader you may find it difficult to deal with larger companies, who may insist on dealing with limited companies. Also, as a sole trader you are inextricably linked to your business – in fact, your business and you are the same legal entity. So if your business fails and owes money (e.g. rent or expenditure on supplies), you are liable for all of your business debts.

Limited company

Limited companies are legal entities – considered by law to be separate from their owners. So by creating a limited company you separate yourself from your business. As a limited company you will have to prepare an annual set of accounts, including a balance sheet and profit and loss account. These must be submitted to Companies House and filed for public record. Unless you have some accountancy expertise you'll have to pay an accountant £500–£1500 to prepare these accounts from your books.

Being a limited company involves more administration and tends to be more expensive (mainly because you need to pay an accountant) than being a sole trader. However, the additional burden and costs are often outweighed by the amount you can save in tax. If your freelance earnings are greater than £20,000, a limited company is typically the most tax-efficient way to do business.

Choosing a business name

However you choose to trade, you'll need to pick a trading (or company) name. Your name must be different to existing company names – so Google your choices to make sure you're not stepping on any corporate toes.

brilliant tip

For you, as a freelancer, the main goal is to be understood and recognised. So choose a business name that helps people 'get' what you do, or just use your own name.

Check the availability of web domains when you're thinking about company names. Because of the ubiquity of business websites, few obvious domain names are available – unless you opt for an obscure top-level domain like .tel, .me or .info. Consider what your business name says about you. Names carry personality and tell potential clients lots about you, so make sure your name is saying the right things about you. Don't choose a wacky name if you're in a serious business and trying to appeal to corporations.

> consider what your business name says about you

Creating your company

The method for creating your business identity depends on your preferred legal status.

Trading as ...

If you become a sole trader (self-employed) then you can simply notify HMRC that you are *trading as* a business name. So if your name is Wilson Bignose but you want to trade as RedRum Designs then your official name will be *Wilson Bignose trading as RedRum Designs*.

Limited company creation

To create your limited company you'll need the help of a company formation agent. Many businesses offer company formation services, so while it is technically something you can do yourself, it's sensible to pay £20–£100 and have it done properly. Company formation is quick and easy – so you can have your company created in a day.

Business bank accounts

Your business must have its own bank account. If you choose to go limited then you must create a new bank account for your limited company – even if you have an existing business account for your sole trader business.

Accountants

Sole traders can spend as little as a few hundred pounds to have an accountant process their books – or they can do it all themselves for no cost at all. Limited company accounts are more time-consuming, so expect to pay £500–£1500 to an accountant each year. If you use a book-keeping system or a spreadsheet that your accountant can work with then you can minimise their work and reduce their charges. If you want to give your accountant a sack full of receipts and have them do all the hard work then expect to pay more.

Basic book-keeping

You can do as little or as much book-keeping as you like. Maintaining accurate financial records takes a little time, but it rewards your efforts by giving you a clear snapshot of your business performance. Well-kept books will show you your sales, profit, expenses, unpaid invoices and debts in an instant – so you always know your financial position. We look at book-keeping and accounts in greater detail in Part 5.

Insurance

As a sole trader you're not obliged to take out any kind of professional insurance. While there are many kinds of insurance available, two types are popular with freelancers: professional indemnity and public liability. Most freelancers get started without any kind of insurance, but choose to take out a policy once their business grows. Some companies insist that all their suppliers have professional indemnity and public liability insurance before they join their preferred supplier lists – so be prepared to get insurance if you work with bigger clients.

> be prepared to get insurance if you work with bigger clients

Professional indemnity insurance

Protect yourself from ... well, *yourself*. Professional indemnity insurance is mandatory for some kinds of professionals – such as financial advisers, architects and accountants – whose advice could lead their clients astray. So this is insurance that protects you from being sued by the clients you've screwed. If you sell knowledge or advice and your clients make important or risky decisions based on your advice, professional indemnity insurance may help you sleep at night.

Public liability insurance

If clients will be visiting your home or office then it's sensible to have public liability insurance. Without insurance you could find yourself with big bills if a client is injured by you or your business while on your premises.

Finding an insurer

Check the British Insurance Broker's Association website (**http://biba.org.uk**) to find a reputable insurance broker.

Professional Contractors Group

The Professional Contractors Group (PCG) is the main professional association for freelancers and contractors. PCG is probably the biggest single voice in the freelance world, and it also offers contract templates, tax investigation insurance and access to discounted services.

Don't sweat the small stuff

Freelancing is your chance to shed the trappings of regular employment, so don't let this talk of company formations and book-keeping put you off. As a freelancer you will spend the majority of your time finding work and completing work.

Book-keeping and administration will consume a fraction of your time – unless you happen to love accounts and admin.

Never forget that as a freelancer, you are free. You can work in your pants, dangling from the ceiling while smoking a pipe and stroking a dachshund, if that's how you do your best work. Remember just how free you are. Now, let's go to work.

 **brilliant** recap

- Take the time to understand the differences between being a limited company and a sole trader before you choose. Ask other freelancers why they chose their legal status, and whether they would choose differently given the chance.

- Choose a business name that communicates something about you – try to choose a name that can grow with you.

- Use spreadsheets or state-of-the-art software, but keep orderly financial records so you can monitor your performance.

- Insurance is essential for some freelancers – and a reassuring luxury for many others.

- Relax – freelancing is fun!

Recommended reading

- Professional Contractors Group (PCG) – **www.pcg.org.uk**
- Freelance Advisor – **www.freelanceadvisor.co.uk**
- Freelance UK – **www.freelanceuk.com**

PART 2

Finding freelance work: how to find the most profitable and manageable work

Almost everything comes from almost nothing.

Henri Frédéric Amiel

Freelancers face two main challenges. You must:

1 Find work.
2 Do work.

All other challenges are peripheral. If you can do these two things, you'll go far. In Part 3 we look at the 'do work' side of freelancing, but before you do anything else, let's find some work.

CHAPTER 6

Take your ass to market

Marketing has a bad reputation ... or as the comedian Bill Hicks famously said, 'If you are in marketing or advertising, kill yourself.' The inventor Edwin Land was no more positive: 'Marketing is what you do when your product is no good.'

But before you abandon this chapter in disgust, let's look at what these two quotes tell us. Bill Hicks is really railing against bad businesses. He was angry about ruthless, immoral businesses that forgo decency in favour of profit. The marketing and advertising departments of evil corporations do not dictate the evil that occurs within – they merely take the evil to market. The second quote makes a great point – that if your product or service is great then you can (theoretically) excel in business with no marketing at all. In reality, even if your product is amazing, and significantly better than your competitors, you'll still need marketing to get an initial client base. For many freelancers, their objective is not to be remarkable, but to be reliable, professional and consistent in the delivery of a premium service.

Don't think of 'marketing' as a nefarious activity conducted by spivs and double-glazing companies. Marketing means to take your goods to market. If you were a farmer, you would take your sheep or your harvest to market. Without the market you would sell nothing. You would not consider farmers evil

without the market you would sell nothing

for taking their wares to the market, so don't consider yourself evil for doing the same. As a freelancer you have services instead of sheep, but you still need to take your services to market before anyone can buy them.

Stop worrying and learn to love the marketing

Embrace marketing, because it's the one thing that really divides successful freelancers from those who struggle or fail. You're selling yourself, so you can choose your methods, choose your messages and choose your objectives. Don't feel trapped into dull corporate marketing modes – be yourself! And be proud of your marketing, because it has more in common with the farmer's seasonal schlep to market than the million-pound marketing campaigns conducted by corporations.

 **brilliant** definition

Marketing
All the activities involved in the transfer of goods from a seller to a buyer, including pricing, advertising, delivery and selling.

What are you selling?

Before you head off to market with your sheep, you need to understand what you're selling. Sure, you know you've got a sheep, but do you know why your clients are buying your sheep? There's a difference between what we sell and what our clients buy. We sell services; clients buy *benefits*. Or as Simon Booth-Lucking puts it, 'Look for the pain. You're like paracetamol and you're looking for your client's pain. Your clients pay you to take the pain away.'

You sell:	Your client buys:
Graphic design	A better-looking business that can help them achieve greater success
Search engine optimisation	More sales through their website
Lawnmowers	Shorter grass and neater lawns
Computer repairs	More efficient computers that help them work
PA services	A life with less stress

 **brilliant** tip

Develop your elevator pitch. Your elevator pitch is a way of explaining what you do, quickly. It should be short enough that you can deliver it during a brief ride in a lift, but complete enough so that anyone who hears it can understand it. Write down your elevator pitch and have it ready in the back of your mind, but always adapt it to your audience. Know how to give a quick overview of your work, but also know how to deviate from it – otherwise you'll sound like an automaton.

Be different

If you're becoming a freelancer in a crowded market then consider being *different*. Look for missed opportunities – things that other freelancers aren't doing. Provide a better service, be more professional, shout about the things everyone else is being quiet about, or add complementary services that make you stand alone among your peers. Think about how you can be more useful to your clients. For example, if you're the only freelance illustrator who can also take photographs, or prepare your illustrations for the web, then you'll be the automatic choice for many clients.

Being different can also be about the *way* you work. Let's imagine that all your peers dress like teenagers and behave like petulant princesses – if you turn up looking organised and work with a cool, professional demeanour, then your clients will love you and your peers will struggle to compete. Don't be afraid to disrupt industry norms and work in the way that feels real and right to you.

brilliant tip

Hedge your bets and never rely on one client, industry, technology or format for your work. It's a common scenario that often leaves freelancers in the merde: you're kept busy by one client, doing one type of work every day for years. Other freelancers envy you, while you pity them for the amount of marketing they have to do. Then, your one client goes bust, you lose everything, and find yourself with no clients, no contacts, a weak portfolio and no marketing momentum. Don't let this happen to you. Don't let one client monopolise your time, because you're the one who is ultimately losing out. Even if you have a corporate sugar daddy, go looking for other jobs, build your web presence and get acquainted with your local business scene.

Specialise

Instead of being just another freelance photographer, in a field of 500, be a freelance pet photographer, in a field of five. Instead of just being a freelance journalist, find a niche, become an expert and write about the things you know and love. Instead of being just another freelance programmer, be one of the rare few that program in your preferred language – and be an expert in that language. Specialising makes your marketing easier to do, and it will help you choose the right kind of work.

When you start freelancing it's tempting to accept any work you are offered, even if it's wrong for you, your skills and your portfolio. This is fine for starters, but as you grow into your free-lance career you'll learn what kind of work is good for you, good for your career and good for your clients. When work levels dip, you may again be tempted by potboiler jobs – projects that won't change your life but will pay your bills – and that's absolutely fine. Do what makes sense.

---
do what makes sense

Specialising takes nerve, because you'll feel that you're excluding work opportunities and reducing your options. And you are. Hold your nerve and stick tight to your specialism and you'll discover that you get better work, have happier clients, become truly expert and spend less time on work you hate for clients you loathe. Oh, and by specialising you can earn more too.

brilliant tip

Take the advice of Jacky and Tim Misson from Rise Sales Development: work out who your ideal customer is and deliberately seek that type of client. 'Your ideal customer wants to buy the very thing that you want to sell. Your ideal customer likes your terms and they like your price. Your ideal customer is easy and profitable.'

brilliant recap

- Marketing yourself can be enjoyable – remember that you're a one-man band, not McEvil Inc.
- Understand the benefits that your services and skills confer to your clients.

▶

● If you spot a gap in your local freelance market, don't be afraid of filling it.

● While it can be useful to specialise, be wary of boxing yourself into a dwindling market, and resist becoming dependent on a small number of clients.

● Decide who you want to work with. Who are your ideal customers?

CHAPTER 7

Find work fast

Finding work is the biggest challenge you face. There are millions of potential clients out there, but they don't know you exist. To begin with, you need to let the world know you're here, and you're ready to work.

Marketing methods vary in their ease, expense, directness and value. Some marketing methods are easy, but they're also unlikely to bring much of a return. Complex, costly marketing methods might bring rich rewards but they'll diminish your wallet and absorb your time. As a new freelancer you're likely to be cash-poor and time-rich, so the ideal marketing method for you is one that takes your time but not your money. So, what is this freely available, valuable, direct but time-consuming marketing method?

The power of the humble telephone call

The most direct way to find work is by calling your potential clients. A phone call is all it takes. All you need is a phone. You don't need a website, a fancy logo or a new suit. You just need a phone. Your phone is a direct line to freelance work. But before you rush off and start calling prospects, let's do some groundwork.

Who needs your services?

Work out who you're selling to. Are your services aimed at general businesses, or are you selling to a particular sector? Are you looking for new businesses, old businesses, big businesses or small businesses? Will you work directly with your end-clients or will you be employed by agencies, consultants or other intermediaries?

 **action**

Identify your clients and their key needs

You may have a few different client groups, so let's identify them and define what they want from you. For each type of client, think about who they are, why they'll hire you and how they'll look for you.

Fill in the blanks below, following these examples.

As a <u>home owner</u>, we want a <u>plumber</u> because we need <u>help fitting a new</u> <u>bathroom</u>. We'll look for our <u>plumber</u> by <u>searching in the Yellow Pages</u>.

As a <u>small business</u>, we need a <u>freelance project manager</u> <u>to help manage</u> <u>a one-off project that's outside our usual remit</u>. We'll look for our <u>freelance</u> <u>project manager</u> by <u>searching online</u>.

As a _____ we want a _____

because we _____. We'll look for our

_____ by _____.

This profiling exercise will give you a clearer picture of the people and businesses that need your services, and how they might look for you. You may need more than one profile if you have different client types. Use this profile to plan your marketing activities – making sure that your tactics bring you closer to your prospects in the places they're already looking.

 **definition**

Prospect

The people who might become clients. It's an awful word, but it's useful as a way to describe the people you want to work with, or enquirers who aren't quite clients yet.

List your potential clients

Now that you've identified the *types* of companies you can work for, you can start building a list of *examples*. Search online and check your local Chamber of Commerce or professional associations to find businesses that fit your profile. Be organised, and put the business names into a spreadsheet, with their phone numbers and contact names in another column.

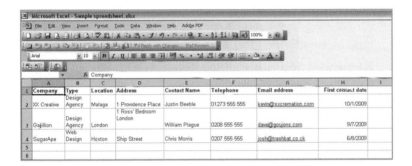

Prepare to call your future clients

Unsolicited phone calls are never popular. So as you prepare to make unsolicited phone calls, you may feel a vague sense of dread, or as though you're committing a crime. You must remember that you're not selling double glazing, and you're not going to call random businesses to offer them something they don't need. By profiling your clients, you know there's a strong chance that the people you call will need you; maybe not today or tomorrow, but one day these businesses will be glad you called.

Because unsolicited calls are unpopular, take steps to minimise your intrusion. Make it easy for people to like you. Don't call at 9:00 on Monday morning, when everyone is trying to wake up and deal with last week's disasters. Don't call at 5:00 on Friday, when everyone is lazily preparing next week's disasters. And don't call at lunch time, when everyone is ... well, eating lunch.

> make it easy for people to like you

Before you call, know exactly what you want to say:

- **Know your goal.** Would you like to meet the client, or do you just want to email them your CV or portfolio? You may find that the shortest, most effective call is one where you briefly introduce yourself, explain what you do and then offer to email more detailed information about yourself.

- **Know who you want to speak to.** Try to find the name of your ideal contact from their website, but if names aren't available then say something like, 'Can I please speak to the person in charge of hiring freelancers?' Try to get the right person on the phone before you deliver your spiel.

- **Know what you want to say.** Write down your script and rehearse it. Know exactly *why* you're calling and *what* you want to achieve. Otherwise you won't know if the call was a success. Having a script and a goal helps you be efficient and it reduces the chances of you wasting the prospect's time. So don't think of a script as being an artificial device that reduces the exchange to a robotic interaction – it's just a guideline that helps you respect people's time.

An approach to calling prospects

Open a phone call with something short and simple like, 'Hi, I'm Ed Wood and I'm just starting out as a freelance _____ in your area. Do you ever use freelance _____?' Cold calling isn't about being a hotshot salesperson; it's about making gentle introductions to new people who are likely to need your help.

Smile when you talk, because your facial expression carries down the wires. Don't tense up and deliver a stilted script with a tight grimace, because your clients will hear that. Smile, relax and be friendly. Remember that you're calling these people to offer something useful.

Stand. Your body is your voice, so make your voice richer, deeper and more relaxed by standing when you speak.

If you feel anxious about calling the contacts on your list, start the day with vigorous exercise. Go running. Go to the gym. Run up and down the stairs 50 times. Release your stress and relax your voice. Don't rely on coffee or cigarettes for relaxation because they're both stimulants and will only raise your anxiety levels. Have a glass of water on hand in case your mouth dries up. Now get calling!

And remember, if you're scared about calling people, what's the worst that could happen? Stop and think about what you're afraid of. Are you worried about people responding rudely to your calls? Are you worried that people will dislike you for calling? Imagine the very worst outcome. The very worst scenario is that you call a company that isn't relevant – and that is not interested in your services. So in the very worst case scenario, you can just apologise sincerely, say toodle-pip, and end the call. And life goes on.

> what's the worst that could happen?

 example

A sample cold-calling script

Receptionist: 'Hello, Metaphysical Widgets...'

Freelancer: 'Hi, could I please speak to the person in charge of hiring freelance engineers?'

Receptionist: 'Sure, I'll put you through.'

Client contact: 'Hi – I'm Sandra, I'm the project manager at MW. How can I help?'

Freelancer: 'Hi Sandra, my name is Dave Jones and I'm a local freelance engineer. I recently became available and just wanted to introduce myself, in case you had a need for an engineer.'

Client: 'Well, hello. Thanks for calling. We don't need any additional help right now, but we occasionally use freelancers.'

Freelancer: 'Great – do you mind if I email over my contact details?'

Client: 'That would be perfect. Can you also send over some details of your past experience, or a CV or something ...?'

Freelancer: 'Of course. I'll send you some information. What's your email address?'

The follow-up – get personal

After each call, do what you agreed during the call. Each prospect will want something different, so while you should have a standard CV or portfolio to attach to your follow-up emails, customise the email to feature the contact's name, something relevant to your conversation and something that connects their business with your services ('Because I specialise in working with technology companies like yours, there's a great fit between my services and your products') – that proves your email is not a generic template sent to thousands of random companies.

Update your spreadsheet too, noting who you spoke to, when you contacted them, and how you followed up. You may make a second batch of calls in the future, so having a record of these interactions may prevent you bothering the same person twice, or forgetting an important detail.

Coping with rejection

If you are friendly, warm, polite and efficient when you call clients, you will mostly get a positive response. If anyone objects to your call, simply apologise and get off the call quickly and politely. Don't expect every phone call to lead to a job, but trust that these calls represent a solid start to your marketing campaign.

The value of calling people

Okay, so calling people isn't easy. It really isn't. Few people choose to call a random stranger when it's so easy to send emails. We can tickle our keyboards and fling any old message into a gazillion inboxes. It's easy. It's not scary. But calling is different. It's personal, it's direct and it's real. And therein lies its power.

Because every aspiring freelancer sends dozens of emails to prospects, emails are as good as worthless. If you want to waste some time but feel like you're doing some great marketing, send lots of unsolicited emails to random companies. If you get a response it will be a minor miracle. Calling people is effective because it's hard and less aspiring freelancers will not do it. Clients like freelancers who show *willingness* – and sending a random email shows nothing but timidity and laziness. Show them you care – pick up the phone!

> clients like freelancers who show willingness

 **brilliant** recap

- Finding work is the biggest challenge you face as a freelancer.
- You can leapfrog the competition by calling your potential clients.
- Identify your ideal clients.
- Plan your phone calls – what will you say, and who will you say it to?
- Smile when you speak, and be friendly – even if you get a negative response.
- Congratulate yourself for taking the direct approach – it will pay off!

CHAPTER 8

Networking: the power of people

N etworking is a big thing – it's more than meetings, more than conferences, more than business cards and more than suits. Networking is not an event, but a long-term endeavour. Don't think of networking as a way to get work; think of networking as a way to make friends. Freelancers need friends. You need friends for support, for sympathy, for advice, for help and for making connections.

What to expect from networking events

Networking opportunities come in many guises. But let's look at some examples to give you an idea of what to expect.

Old school networking with dudes in suits

At some networking events you will encounter a room full of suited business people, all replete with business cards, all eager to sell. Old school networkers are more likely to want to work the room and more likely to focus on swapping elevator pitches and business cards. If you have a service that's needed by a general business audience, this type of networking could be very useful, but you may have to tolerate the stuffy atmosphere and occasionally outmoded thinking.

New school networking

Many modern business people have dropped the suits in favour of jeans and trainers. And modern networking is more relaxed too – favouring friendly settings and the chance to meet new people in an informal environment. Modern networkers are more likely to have forgotten their business cards – if they even own any – and are more likely to want to know about you as well as your business.

Networking with a small 'n'

Great networking opportunities – where you can really get to know the people in your network, arise unexpectedly. As Will McInnes, MD of social media agency Nixon McInnes noted, 'We like networking with a little "n" – the worst networking opportunities are always called "Networking".' Incidental networking opportunities can be found at conferences, workshops, meet-ups and socials.

Don't go out selling

Networking is the process of building connections between you and the people around you. So when you go to a conference, or a networking event, or a party – don't feel like you're trying to sell yourself to everyone you meet. If you focus on selling you're likely to miss the nice things that happen when people get together – like smiles, laughs and serendipity. Just relax, listen to the people you meet and ask a few questions.

> don't feel like you're trying to sell yourself

But I'm scared!

You're not the only one. Very few people are born networkers. I wrestled with my anxiety for weeks before taking the plunge. Anna Bertmark had a similar aversion to networking, so she tackled it head-on by doing public speaking training with Toastmasters International. Anna can now enter a room full of strangers with confidence. Anna's approach to dealing with problems is, to me, the epitome of the ideal freelance character: go-getting, self-starting and ready for change.

brilliant dos and don'ts

Networking is what you make it. For happy networking:

Do

✔ Be inquisitive. Try to learn about the people behind the businesses they represent.

✔ Take business cards, but only get them out when someone asks for them.

✔ Question the value of networking events. It's dangerously easy to lose time chatting to nice people – but remember that you're on company time. If you can't see any potential value from the meetings, try another group.

✔ Become a regular. If a networking event has potential, you'll need to turn up regularly and get to know people.

✔ Look for ways to be helpful. Instead of viewing every person as a potential client, think first about how you can be helpful, or how you can connect your contacts to each other.

Don't

✘ Expect immediate results. Networking is about building relationships, not winning instant work.

✘ Be too eager to foist your business card on people. If you want to exchange details with someone, ask for their card. They'll probably reciprocate.

✘ Act desperate. You may be gagging for a job, but never let it show. Desperation is deeply unattractive.

✘ Look over the shoulder of the person you're talking to, in search of someone more interesting. Some networkers believe the 'right' way to behave at a networking event is to flit from person to person, exchange a quick elevator pitch, swap cards, and then look for the next person to dally with. But to

▶

others this approach is anathema – it's the very worst kind of interaction, reducing the potential of human cooperation to a kind of corporate prostitution. So unless your hero is Gordon Gekko, be a patient, friendly, inquisitive networker and let the benefit of networking build gradually, forgetting the potential rewards as you make new friends.

Choose your networking groups

Networking groups abound. Unless you're in a small village, far from towns and cities, there should be networking groups near you. Try a few different types to discover what you enjoy and what you find useful. You may prefer:

- **Niche networking** with a specific kind of business – where do your *clients* meet?
- **General business networking** – meeting anyone and everyone.
- **Peer networking** – getting to know professionals like you.
- **Freelance networking** – meeting other freelancers in all kinds of professions and industries.
- **Relaxed networking** – casual, evening meet-ups in pubs as opposed to more formal daytime events.

Create your own group

If you want a networking group that doesn't exist, create it! I wanted to meet more writers, so I created WriteClub – a group specifically for writers that now meets in two cities.

Thanks to the web, and websites like Twitter, WordPress, Google Groups, Facebook and Meetup, it's very easy to create a community.

brilliant recap

● Networking is a process rather than an event.

● Networking can happen anywhere – so get used to looking for opportunities in all kinds of clubs and groups.

● Don't go to networking events to sell – go to learn and make friends.

● It's normal to be nervous about networking, but with a bit of practice you'll soon enjoy it.

● Find local networking opportunities or start a new group.

CHAPTER 9

Get a website

G et a website. Any website will do, but get a website. *Now.*

Why you need a website

Thanks to a bunch of interconnected computers, the world is less mysterious. When we need to know, we just search. Your employers, colleagues, peers, contacts and clients will all be Googling you. When they search, they want to find evidence of your existence – they want supporting evidence that you are more than a name, more than the CV on their desk. They search for evidence, clues, history, character, personality and nuance. Your competitors are already online – offering rich insights into themselves. If you are not there, you are effectively deselecting yourself from the competition.

'If we can't find *something* about a freelancer online, we won't use them. It's as simple as that. No web presence? Fine, we move on to the next candidate. It's impossible for us to evaluate a freelancer if they're not online.'

Darren Fell, MD, Crunch

Don't delay the process of getting a website. Start small, start cheap, start fast. Build. Develop. Improve. Start with something scrappy and make it better as time and money affords. It's infinitely better to have a modest website online than it is to have no website at all. Don't fall into the trap of waiting for your website to be perfect before you launch. If a client searches for you,

start small, start cheap, start fast

they're looking for information, not a mind-blowing digital experience. Of course, if websites are your business then your site must look good, but don't let lofty ambitions stop you from launching your site. The quest for perfection can lead you to paralysis.

Key features for your website

Keep it simple, but make sure you include the information your clients and contacts will come looking for.

Be clear about your identity

You may have a snappy business name, but make sure your own name is still visible and obvious to anyone who visits your site.

Skills and services

Write about the services you offer and the skills you have. Write confidently, positively and clearly about the work you do.

Portfolio and experiences

Show off your work, and write about the experiences that make you an outstanding freelancer.

Clients

Reassure your visitors by showing them that you've been working with other people. Your clients don't have to be international brands – all clients are good clients.

Testimonials

Testimonials are another way to offer *social proof* – reassuring evidence that you have worked with other clients. Testimonials are also a great way to break up your own copy. Instead of making lots of bold statements about yourself, why not let your clients speak for you?

About you

Give visitors a hint of the real you. Whether you do that with irreverent copy or an informal photo, make sure you show people that you're a real human being and not a freelance droid.

Contact details

Don't be shy. You want people to call you, email you, assail you with interesting projects – hell, anything at all! Include your email address, a phone number and details about your location. If you're worried about spam, use an email program with a better spam filter. As a freelancer, you need to be contactable. Don't lose work because you insist on hiding behind a contact form.

> as a freelancer, you need to be contactable

For those about to start ...

Okay, so you're wondering how to include a portfolio or testimonials if you're just starting out. That's simple: you don't. Your website is an organic thing – it grows as you grow and goes where you go. So start small and add these elements when you have them.

How to write about yourself

Writing about yourself can be agonising process. How do you confidently sell yourself without sounding conceited? How do you sound friendly, modest and professional all at once? Where do you start?

There is no right way to write about yourself, but here are a few pointers:

- **Be honest**. Don't make claims that you can't back up. Don't be tempted to exaggerate, because savvy clients will see right through it.

- **Avoid hyperbole**. Instead of saying vague and clichéd statements like 'world-class' or 'cutting-edge' when describing your skills or experiences, write plainly and simply. If you catch yourself using 'very' a lot – cut it out!

- **Be positive**. Give readers a positive experience by writing about yourself in positive terms. Avoid criticisms, negative comments or anything remotely snide. Many negative statements can be rephrased in positive terms: for example, 'I have never had a disappointed client' is loaded with negativity – far better as 'My clients are always delighted with my work'.

- **Ask for feedback**. Get a friend to read over your words. Listen to their feedback objectively. Don't take it personally but think about how their feedback can improve your writing.

- **Remember your reader**. With every word that you write, think about your intended reader, and how the words will make them feel. Your writing has an objective – keep this in mind while you write.

 **example**

Here's an example of a profile that is clear and simple, but effective too.

James Ensall – freelance web and graphic designer
Since 2001 I've been designing visual identities, online and offline, for small and medium-sized businesses. After studying graphic design at university I spent five years with M&P Associates, designing web and print identities for many high-profile clients, including Amstrad and Nivea.

How can I help?
If you need a new logo, print design or website refresh, give me a call. I specialise in designing websites that are carefully aligned to your brand, and designed to perform. Because I understand search engine optimisation (SEO) I can help you reach a wider audience and increase sales online.

Barter your way to a web presence

One of the surprising, unseen benefits of freelancing is that you suddenly have a skill that can be traded and swapped. Skills swaps are popular among freelancers and can be the perfect way to get things done when you have more time than money. To get a website in exchange for your services, keep your eyes wide open for a web designer who might need your help.

brilliant tip

Skills swaps are a great way to get things done, but make sure you and your swapper have a clear understanding of the arrangement. Make sure the agreement is detailed in writing – even if it's just in a series of emails between you both. For tax purposes, you must both raise invoices for the work you do, even if they remain unpaid because they cancel each other out.

Let work find you – through your website

You can find work in a million different ways, but your own website has certain advantages over other marketing methods. Your website is a giant billboard that costs nearly nothing but is visible to everyone, wherever they are in the world. If you think about it, that's incredible. Websites cost very little, but are visible to everyone. So while most marketing methods are limited to your networks, or the distances you can cover with ads, emails and calls, your website is *unlimited* in its potential. Your website can reach people that you don't know. Your website can reach people that you don't know *and start selling to them* – and it can do it while you're sleeping. Thanks to your website, you could be landing your best, most interesting client while you dream about riding a three-legged unicorn through a field of cheese. The potential and power of the web is hard to overstate.

Effective websites take time. New websites are like baby birds. They're weak, vulnerable and unlikely to take off. Websites need time to grow, to mature and develop into something significant. Maintain your website by regularly checking the content. Is it relevant? Is it all correct and working properly? Do you have any new information to add to it? Can you update your blog? Can you add more portfolio pieces, client names or testimonials?

The basics of search engine optimisation

As you know, search engines are the way we navigate the web. So you need to align your website with the way people search for people like you. Get it? Search engine optimisation (SEO) can get complicated, but the basics are very simple: if you want to be found when people search for 'freelance ventriloquist' make sure your website includes the words 'freelance ventriloquist'. Simple.

There are two main factors that dictate where your website appears in search results: your *content* and the number of *links* to your site from other sites.

Optimise your content

Being found online is immensely valuable because every visitor is a potential client. So spend a little time thinking about how people will search for you and what keywords they will type into their preferred search engine.

Build a list of relevant keywords

1 Write down all the keywords you can think of. Your keywords should be the words and phrases that people would use to search for you. So, if you're a freelance project manager, your keywords include 'freelance project manager', 'freelance project management' and maybe 'freelance project managers [location]'. Think about how other people refer to your services, and make sure you use those words on your website.

2 Look at your competitors' websites. What keywords are they using in their page titles and headings? In many browsers you can use Control + U to view the source code of the website – this will give you a clearer view of the meta description (see next page) and meta keywords. Meta titles are displayed in the top bar of your browser window.

3 Put all your keywords into Google's Keyword Tool. Google will suggest other relevant keywords – but don't assume Google's suggestions are all correct. It is worth using Google's Keyword Tool because it may suggest good keywords that you hadn't thought of, but don't be surprised if it has nothing new to offer.

Use your keywords in your website

Use relevant keywords when it makes sense to use them. Never stuff your website with an abundance of keywords, because even if Google sends people your way, your visitors will think you're suffering from some kind of mania. Your website must appeal to search engines and human visitors in equal measure, so don't woo one in spite of another. Write naturally about your services, using the relevant keywords as required. If possible, feature keywords in your page titles, headings and body copy.

Meta data

Websites are made of code. Every website includes invisible information, called meta data. Think of meta data as information about information – or a way of classifying stuff. Make sure your website has full and complete meta titles, meta keywords and meta descriptions – but never stuff them full of keywords.

Links

If your website is great, people will share it with their own audience by linking to it. Links are like a vote of confidence and links are how search engines calculate your website's importance. Amazing sites that are useful and popular have lots of links. Link building is an art form that you could spend years exploring – or you could just concentrate your efforts on building a great website with useful content. For example, if you write blockbuster blog posts that attract attention, links will follow.

> link building is an art form

brilliant tip

Get a few quick links to your website from:

● Google Local
● web directories
● your social media profiles (add links from Flickr, Twitter, Facebook, etc.)
● professional associations you belong to
● friends' blogs.

Expand your web presence with social media

Social websites that create communities and the spaces for online conversations can be immensely valuable for freelancers. Social networks, forums and email groups offer:

● virtual colleagues
● friends on demand
● informal networking.

brilliant definition

Social media
Websites and other media that allow social interaction. Blogs, social networks, forums, email lists and micro-blogging platforms are all social media.

Social media can help you find work, but approach online spaces with care and enter them with a spirit of friendly cooperation.

brilliant dos and don'ts

When exploring social media:

Do

- ✔ Observe. Don't contribute until you've observed and understood the rules of engagement.
- ✔ Be nice. If people are snarky, rise above it.
- ✔ Be helpful. Look for ways to share your knowledge or connect people to new ideas.
- ✔ Be patient. Don't expect to be everyone's best friend instantly.

Don't

- ✘ Barge in and start selling your wares.
- ✘ Over-share. Think carefully before posting a message. Would you say the same thing to your favourite client, or your mother?
- ✘ React to rudeness. It's better (and easier) to ignore unpleasant people.
- ✘ Forget to look for community rules. Many forums and email lists have clear guidelines for participation.

If you're unfamiliar with websites like Twitter and you shy away from forums or email lists – give them a try. If you don't like it, you can easily leave. There's a good chance you'll enjoy interacting online, and the potential benefits are undeniable. More and more conversations happen online. Deals are made. Alliances are forged. Trends are set. Real world events are instigated and entire memes erupt, expand and expire in a matter of hours. If you want to keep up with your peers and your clients, visit the places where they congregate, lest you miss out.

> more and more conversations happen online

A strategy for social media

The size and scope of social media are massive, so you may feel daunted by the idea of diving in. Where to start? How to begin? If you're overwhelmed by the enormity of social media, start *local*.

Look for local groups, local people, people you know, people you've heard of. Use the websites and groups that other locals are using. When you're networking, ask for recommendations of useful online groups. Rather than hanging out online with a bunch of random castaways from every corner of the interweb, gather around people you know.

Get familiar

All the stuff you do online will benefit your freelance career. Whether you're helping people find you, making friends, developing contacts, or sharing your expertise, your time is well spent. Don't feel you have to achieve everything at once though; start small and gradually feel your way around.

 **brilliant** recap

● Get a website.

● Your website can bring you valuable job opportunities.

● Make sure your website clearly shows your contact details.

● Write about yourself honestly, avoiding hyperbole but remaining positive.

● Understand the essence of SEO because search engines are your link to all the clients you haven't yet met.

● Dabble with social media, because important conversations are happening online.

CHAPTER 10

Blog for victory

B logs are so ridiculously common that it's easy to feel there's just no point in having one. Remarkably, in spite of their ubiquity, blogs offer clear benefits to freelancers, including:

- **A voice.** Your website may be comprehensive, but how much *personality* does it contain? Does your website give you a space to release your personality? Blogs are useful because they are a less pressured online space, a place where opinions are allowed and conversation is encouraged.

- **Connections.** Bloggers inhabit a community, irritatingly called the Blogosphere. Having a blog lets you join discussions and take your place in industry debates. You can demonstrate your knowledge and show people that you are keeping up with developments.

- **SEO-juice.** With a blog attached to your main website you get the SEO benefit of regularly updated content. Search engines love fresh content because they believe it indicates relevant, useful information. With regular blog posts your website will rush up the search results, you'll get more hits, and then you can take over the world.

How to blog well

Bloggers fit broadly into two main categories: there are those for whom the blog is the business and their main aim is to profit by blogging. Then there's everyone else: people who blog as an adjunct to their primary activities, people who blog to record their thoughts or share their discoveries. For now, you're likely to fall into the latter category. If you discover that blogging is your thing and work feels like a chore, by all means pursue blogging. Dedicated, talented bloggers can certainly earn a living online.

The following advice is aimed squarely at the casual blogger – the kind of person who wants to benefit from blogging, but isn't expecting to change the world or be read by millions worldwide.

Give away everything you know

Just before I went freelance, I had the good fortune to meet two web developers, Michael Bailey and Premasagar Rose, who gave me advice that I have acted on ever since: 'Give away everything you know, and you will receive back more than you ever had.'

I listened to their advice with my dubious hat on. Coming from a traditional corporate environment, where the general mood was one of selfish competition, their advice was deeply contrary to my received wisdom. Trade secrets were to be jealously guarded, even when they didn't really exist. The idea of giving information away, and being open and honest with knowledge, seemed downright dangerous. But Michael and Premasagar were so generous with their own knowledge that I decided to try out their approach. And I haven't looked back.

Of course, there are things that I choose to keep quiet about, such as commercially sensitive details like prices or projects. And I'm very, very careful with my client's information. But in terms of my skills, my discoveries and my thoughts, I give them away freely. I've shared my best advice on freelancing and copywriting with all kinds of random strangers – on blogs and in person. I've even shared the secrets of my modest success with direct competitors, determined to open up, even when I sometimes wonder what the hell I'm doing.

Giving away what you know is a liberating experience, and while it might sound like a purely philanthropic enterprise, it has an uncanny knack of bringing greater treasures your way. Giving your knowledge freely will earn you many admirers: people who will respect you as an informed, intelligent individual; people who will feel indebted for the knowledge you shared; and people who will admire your selflessness. By *giving* knowledge, you also open yourself to *receive* knowledge, and you create a role for yourself as an active, thoughtful member of your community.

> by *giving* knowledge, you also open yourself to *receive* knowledge

I know what you're thinking. You're worried that if you give away your big ideas or the secret of your success, another freelancer will copy your methods and nab your jobs. Okay, there's a teeny-weeny chance this might happen, but it's as likely as winning the Euro jumbo lottery twice in one month. Because even if your rival *could* replicate an element of your success, *they can never be you*. No rival can ever do what you do, in the way you do it. Even if they read your every word and follow your every step, they will still be several steps behind. So use your blog to give away your knowledge. Don't hold back.

Get commenting

Just as the best way to learn to write is by reading, the best way to be a better blogger is by reading blogs. What have your peers got to say? What topics are stirring up the industry? Find out by reading blogs. Don't be afraid of joining the debate by leaving comments. Comments are also great because they're like a little calling card. They let a blogger know that you've been nosing around their website. Comments can also help you lead people back to your own blog. Or you can continue a discussion started by one blogger with a post of your own.

Get reviewed

If writing is not one of your strengths, ask a friend to review your blog posts before you publish them. Good blog posts do not depend on big words or cleverly crafted prose; good blog posts are clear and communicative. Your post should have a central point. If you can't find the point when you read it back, try to recall what the point was and either insert the point or delete the post.

> your post should have a central point

Double-check that your post has a clear message, a clear (rather than clever) title and, if possible, a cute picture of a cat. Well, the cat is optional, but if you can find a picture to brighten up your posts, *do*. Search **www.flickr.com** for pictures with a Creative Commons licence (that means you can use them for free, as long as you attribute them to the owner). Simply use the Advanced Search options, then tick the box for 'Creative Commons-licensed content' and 'Find content to use commercially'.

Hatch a plan

Blogging is hard work. It's not easy to come up with ideas, especially after you've covered all the big, cornerstone pieces. Make it easier by planning your posts in advance. Do a mind-map of topics and schedule when you will cover them. Write a few comprehensive posts and turn them into a series, publishing them in parts over several weeks. If inspiration fails you, consider swapping guest posts with another blogger.

And remember ...

You'll be lucky to get anyone reading your blog, so relax. Write what's on your mind. Let your readers know who you are.

Remain professional (and legal) but don't stress too much about what people might think. Besides, a little controversy never hurt a blogger!

 brilliant recap

- You don't have to attract thousands of readers to make blogging worthwhile. Even if a handful of potential clients read your blog and form a positive view of you, then it's worth it.

- Give away your knowledge. If you want readers to value your blog, give them something of value.

- Make sure every blog post has a clear point.

- Get a friend to review your posts.

- Comment on your peers' blogs, and encourage commenting on your own blog posts (perhaps by asking questions or inviting suggestions).

CHAPTER 11

How to sell

Think about the best shopping experience you've ever had. Did the seller bamboozle you with a well-rehearsed monologue? Or did the seller enquire about your needs? Did the seller make you feel inferior, or like an equal? Did you feel listened to – or did you feel like you were being swept along in the current of a sales pipeline?

Selling is about solving people's problems by giving them things they need at a fair price. Selling is not about deception. A good sale satisfies the needs of both the seller *and* the buyer – leaving both feeling like winners. So in this chapter we'll look at selling, because as a freelancer you will need to sell your services. You can either understand the sales process and improve your chances of winning work, or you can pretend that you're not selling anything and lose a few jobs.

Believe in your product (that's you)

Before you can convince anyone that they should buy you, you need to value yourself. To understand why you're valuable, think about the work you do, and why people hire freelancers like you. What are they trying to achieve? What purpose do you serve? As a freelancer, you're likely to contribute to your client's projects, helping them to improve their own services, deliver a new product or reach a new audience. However you help, your efforts are likely to increase profits for your client. It's easy to value yourself when you understand the value your clients get from you. Be conscious of how you save your clients' time – or of how you do things differently and better than other freelancers. All these factors contribute to your intrinsic value – and it's this value that you're selling. By understanding your own value, you can feel confident and certain when speaking to someone who wants to buy you.

be conscious of how you save your clients' time

brilliant dos and don'ts

When you receive a new enquiry:

Do

✔ Respond quickly.

✔ Think about whether the enquiry is the kind of work you want: are they the right kind of client – or do you just need the work?

✔ Google the enquirer – find out more about them.

✔ Read and re-read the enquiry – what exactly do they want?

✔ Think about how your services match up to their requirements.

✔ Plan your response – can you meet their deadline, can you offer a ballpark cost?

Don't

✗ Send a short, thoughtless email in response to a valuable enquiry (unless you don't want the work).

✗ Respond without reading the email thoroughly.

✗ Pick up the phone before you've thought about what to say.

✗ Make promises you can't keep.

✗ Bend over backwards to get a job you don't want.

brilliant definition

Sales

Selling begins where marketing ends. If marketing is taking your ass to market, selling is the process you go through once the buyer takes an interest in your, ahem, product. So selling is the negotiation and deal-making process that begins once you have a customer interested in your wares.

Ask intelligent questions

Give your clients a happy experience by selling softly. You don't need to pressure anyone into buying – and they're more likely to buy if you give them the space to make their own decisions. One smart way to make your clients feel listened to is to ask intelligent questions. So rather than taking your client's request at face value, ask 'Why?' *Why* do you want a new website? *Why* do you want to change your branding? *Why* do you want to illustrate these documents with dancing donkeys? Never assume you know your client's motives, because you'll often be surprised. By understanding your client's goals you'll be able to propose better solutions and give them a better service.

> never assume you know your client's motives

Educate your clients

Some of your clients will be naive about your industry or profession. You may be a freelance designer working with an industrial plant manufacturer, or you might be a freelance audio engineer working with a medical services company. In many situations, you will be the expert and your client will need some help to understand the way you work, the way you charge and the benefits you offer.

It's okay to ask your client how much they know – and it's totally reasonable for them to know absolutely nothing about your profession. After all, that's why they're hiring you. Gently explain any confusing details of your work. Avoid mysterious TLAs (three-letter acronyms) and other industry jargon. Speak plainly and always relate your services to the benefits they offer. If you can educate your clients, you can empower them to make a wise choice. By being helpful you'll probably win their hearts (and their project) but even if they choose another freelancer they will always think favourably of you.

Attending sales or interview meetings

When you get a new lead, what do you do? Do you conduct lengthy negotiations by email, or do you suggest a meeting? Meeting people takes time, but the benefits are hard to ignore. By meeting your potential clients face to face, you stop being that random freelancer and become flesh, bones and a beating heart.

Meeting people is often the logical next step to follow an enquiry. The client needs you. You want the client. You need to take your relationship to the next level. The best way to do this – distance permitting – is with a meeting. By meeting you also build on the existing momentum – the momentum your client began when they contacted you. You can either seize the day, take up your prospect's cry for help and begin defining their needs, or you can let the fire cool, the momentum fade and the work slip from your grasp. It's your choice.

> take up your prospect's cry for help

The trouble with meetings

Meetings take time. Lots of time. It's easy to lose half a day over a meeting that takes one hour. *How?* Well … you prepare for the meeting, travel there, have the meeting, travel back, debrief and then, at last, you can return to work. So don't go giving away your time to every random caller, because you never know if an enquirer is a genius entrepreneur or a deranged lunatic. I've spent hours talking to potential clients about supposed projects, when what they really needed was a counsellor. Oh, and the supposed projects often fizzle out. So be wary about meeting potential clients, especially if you will be travelling, unless your client wants to pay your travel expenses.

Travelling to meetings

While it's good practice to make yourself available for meetings, you'll probably have to cover the costs. If you're an independent freelancer going to see an enquirer about a project worth £1000 or more, they may think you churlish for demanding £15 for a train ticket. For large companies the administrative nightmare caused by trying to extract £15 from some distant pot of cash being eagerly guarded by an accounts administrator is not worth the benefit of using you. I landed one of my best contracts because I happily attended a meeting, while other contenders were busy demanding cash advances. So there are many benefits to making yourself available for meetings, and you're more likely to win the job if a client can see the real you. But try to talk about money – if only in vague terms – before you arrange a meeting, especially if you suspect the enquirer has a teeny-weeny budget.

brilliant dos and don'ts

When you attend initial meetings with new clients:

Do

✔ Look clean, tidy and organised. If you arrive late at the meeting place and look dishevelled, your client will assume you work in a similar manner.

▶

✔ Know what the meeting is for. Are you going to plan the next stage, or just get an idea of the client's requirements?

✔ Make notes.

✔ Ask questions. Show that your brain is fully engaged by thinking about what your new client is saying and asking for clarification when anything is unclear – or question anything unusual.

✔ Give your client a few ideas. There is a danger they will give your ideas to another freelancer, but it's worth the risk because giving away knowledge shows that you're bright and it's likely to win you the job.

Don't

✘ Let random oddballs monopolise your time.

✘ Give away your work until you know that the enquirer wants to engage you for paid work. It's one thing to give away ideas, quite another to give away your services.

✘ Attend too many unpaid meetings. Account for meetings in your proposal, showing clearly that they are a billable item, not an unending well of fun time that they can draw on whenever they feel like a chat. Your time is money.

✘ Let meetings drag on. When you encounter chatty people who like to digress, rein them in. Interrupt politely and steer the conversation back to the project. You have attended the meeting for a purpose, so make sure you don't leave the meeting without achieving your goals.

Talking about money

Eventually, your sales conversations will turn to money. Putting a price on your head is hard, and saying that price out loud is even harder (perhaps that's part of our traditional British reserve). Thankfully, talking about money gets easier with time. During the early stages of negotiations, a client may ask for a ballpark cost. This indicates that they want a rough idea of your charges – just in case you're too expensive for them. If possible, develop a fast reckoning system for quoting. For example, a web designer might tell clients that a simple site of 5–10 pages costs £500–£1500 depending on the functionality required. A freelance writer might tell clients that they charge £150–£200 per 1000

> if possible, develop a fast reckoning system for quoting

words. If you feel too uncertain about the project to even quote ballpark costs then just tell the client your hourly or daily rate – often that's enough to reassure them that you're within their budget.

Be open about your rates and try to mention them at the start of your relationship, because if your client is expecting to pay a fraction of your charges, there's absolutely no point wasting your time talking about your services and preparing a quote. Mentioning indicative costs like your rate or typical charges is a great way to filter out clients who just can't afford you. There are few things more frustrating than finishing off a promising two-hour meeting with an exciting new client, only to discover they can only afford half an hour of your time.

To dissuade time-wasters or people with micro-projects, you may want to have a minimum charge (for example half a day). Of course, there's nothing intrinsically wrong with tiny projects – just that for some freelancers they're hardly worth the administration involved in setting up a new client, invoicing, chasing payment and so on.

 'People that pay for things never complain. It's the guy you give something to that you can't please.'

Will Rogers

The trouble with small jobs and favours

There's a peculiar phenomenon that strikes the micro-project ... for some reason it's always the low-value projects, the special deals and the freebies that become the most problematic. Whenever you lower your rates, or break your usual rules, or take on something as a favour to a friend, you can guarantee that the client will be the most demanding, ungrateful, unhelpful and uncharitable git you've ever had the misfortune of dealing with. So think twice before you cut your rates for a friend in need.

Follow-up after meetings

After any meeting, send your client an email to confirm the rough details of your discussion. If they're waiting for a quote from you, tell them when they can expect it. Every time you submit a quote, put a note in your diary to follow it up. Without some kind of reminder, you could easily forget all about it. Don't be shy about following up after submitting your quote. After you've invested time and energy in the quote it's perfectly acceptable to see it through.

If a client agrees your quote

Well done! Treat yourself to a biscuit and a sit down. Then send your client a polite email, acknowledging their acceptance and explaining the next steps. Your next steps may be to have a kick-off meeting, to raise an initial invoice or to start work.

If a client haggles over costs

First, establish *why* they are haggling. Why do they think you're too expensive? What are they comparing you with? Clients often compare a trio of quotes, so they may think you're expensive because they're comparing you with an inexperienced student who is offering to work, literally, for peanuts. So try to find out who they're comparing you with. If your competitors are less skilled or less experienced, try to show the client how your higher cost translates to greater benefits.

You may discover that your competitors are all well qualified too, and that your quote is just plain pricey. If you want the job, consider lowering your rates, or try to show the client the differences between you and your competitors. If you have better skills or more experience, then naturally you're going to cost more. If you can afford to lose the job, explain to the client that your higher rates reflect the higher quality service that you offer, and if they prefer to pay less for an inferior service then that is their choice to make. Your client may be entirely motivated by cost, but most clients are looking for a balance between good value and good work.

> show the client the differences between you and your competitors

If a client declines your quote

Bad luck. It happens. Don't feel bad – there are a million possible reasons why you might have lost the job. Luckily there are a billion other projects out there, just waiting for you to find them. Learn from lost jobs. Ask the client why they chose someone else. Be polite and gracious in defeat – there's a good chance the client feels awful about not giving you the work.

 brilliant recap

- Selling involves finding a deal that benefits both the buyer and the seller.
- Understand the value that you are offering your clients.
- Take care when responding to valuable enquiries – unless you don't want the job.

▶

- Make sure you're selling to the right client – the kind of client that will further your career.

- Be inquisitive about your clients' goals – you can often learn things that will improve the service you offer them.

- Talk openly about your typical charges – you might save yourself from wasting time with the wrong sort of client.

Recommended reading

- *Selling the Invisible* by Harry Beckwith (Warner Books, 1997)

- *SPIN Selling* by Neil Rackham (Gower Publishing, 1995)

CHAPTER 12

Get more work than you can handle

Reluctantly you will learn to love the 'peaks and troughs' – the fluctuating levels of work that come with being a freelancer. One week you're swamped with work, raising invoices, batting away enquiries, churning out quotes, completing projects, riding the success pony and feeling like Eddie the Eagle at the height of his fame, and then the next week your diary is bare, your inbox is empty and you feel

freelance fortunes dip and dive

like, well, Eddie the Eagle at the height of his fame. Freelance fortunes dip and dive, and to some extent you can never change that. But there are a few things you can do to iron out the bigger crinkles in your career.

Retainers

If a client wants your help regularly, offer them a *retainer*. Retainers are agreements to pay a certain amount per month to secure a fixed quantity of your time. So your client can then just pick up the phone and get you to do stuff, without worrying about quotes, costs or invoices. You invoice the client for the same amount every month, and they know how much of your time they have to use. Retainers are rightly prized by freelancers for the security they provide. If you secure a retainer, enjoy it but do not rely on it – just in case it (or your client) suddenly vanishes.

Support or maintenance contracts

These are perfect for freelancers who create things that need maintenance or regular updates. You may need to charge a client for something like web hosting, or for a support or maintenance contract. Freelance writers might need to update a website or document regularly, and freelance SEOs can provide monthly reports. Think about how you can be helpful to clients on an ongoing basis.

Relentless marketing

Francesca Papp is a freelance sheep shearer. When she's busy shearing sheep, *she's busy shearing sheep*, and has no time for marketing. So she stops networking, her blog runs dry, she neglects her social networks and the whole world forgets Francesca. When she's done shearing sheep, she realises her inbox is empty and there's no work on the horizon. So Francesca polishes her networking boots, digs out her business cards, dusts off her blog and updates her statuses. Marketing maniacally, Francesca soon finds work. Busy again, Francesca stops marketing and the cycle repeats. And repeats and repeats until the end of time.

When you look for work, you will find work. When you don't look, you don't find – so it's hardly surprising that freelancers experience 'peaks and troughs'. When you're busy you want to focus on the work that pays. You want to keep your clients happy and you want to raise invoices. You don't want to attend yet another networking event, or wrestle with a blog post when you're inundated with work. And that's fine – if you want to live a life of perpetual fluctuation. If you want more than this, if you want a reliable freelance income with less of the terrifying lulls, then you need to maintain your marketing activities, even when you're busy.

> it's hardly surprising that freelancers experience 'peaks and troughs'

Keep your marketing juggernaut moving along – even when you're busy. Slow things down, back off the pace, sure – but do a little something each week. Get out and about, update your blog, spend half an hour on your plan for world domination – but don't let your marketing drop just because you're busy.

How simply being amazing can keep you loaded with work

Good freelancers get lots of work through *referrals*. Their clients, so delighted with the service they received, tell friends and colleagues about this amazing freelancer. Now, there is something special about referrals, something that multiplies their value beyond the usual value of a new client.

First, any client you gain through referral is a client won without marketing – so the cost of acquiring that customer is zilch. Second, a client who approaches you after being recommended by a friend or trusted peer is less likely to seek competing quotes. So many referred clients will land in your lap as a done deal. Because they've heard about you from someone they trust, they don't want to compare you with another freelancer.

So, the obvious question is: *how do you get more referrals?*

Be unbeatable to get more referrals

You will probably get recommendations from the clients who get exactly what they want. Clients who get the work they want, when they want it, delivered with every condition met and a few unexpected bonuses thrown in for free – these are the clients who will sing your praises and recommend you heartily to everyone they meet. Dissatisfied clients are unlikely to recommend you. Hell, even clients who are *just* satisfied are unlikely to recommend you. Your clients will probably require full-on delight before they start talking about you. So that's your goal: total, utter delight.

Delighting clients is not always easy. Clients can be a pain in the backside. They can be difficult and demanding. You can try your best, work like a dog and over-deliver on a project but still get nothing but 'meh' from your client. Your clients are just people, so just as some people struggle to maintain harmonious relationships with others, so too will some of your clients. While it's good practice to strive to please your clients, occasionally projects will go astray, clients will turn nasty and you'll reach a point of no return, where the only sensible course of action is to politely excuse yourself.

> most of your clients will
> be reasonable people

But most of your clients will be reasonable people, and by giving your client a little bit extra – whether that's a little bit more thought, an idea they haven't paid for, an insight they weren't expecting or a just a fraction of work beyond what they're paying for – you can leave them feeling delighted that they picked you.

If you go further than other freelancers, if you can tolerate pedantry and unreasonable demands, if you can accommodate tight deadlines and accomplish seemingly impossible challenges, then you will be the one they remember. And you'll be the one they recommend.

brilliant tip

Jump the job queue by responding to enquiries faster than everyone else. When a new enquiry lands in your inbox, respond immediately. There's a good chance that the same enquiry email has been sent to your rivals. The first freelancer to respond has the best chance of getting the work. Think about it: if you're looking for a freelancer, do you want to hire the attentive, alert, responsive one or the one that took two days to respond to your enquiry? You can leap ahead of your competitors simply by being there, and being there *fast*.

Incentivise referrals

Because referrals are valuable to any business, many companies offer incentives to people who send work their way. You could offer clients 10 per cent of the project value for every referral, or a flat £100 fee. Or you could offer the referrer some of your time as a thank-you. Go crazy and print loyalty cards and stamp them every time a referrer sends you a new client. When their card is full, give them something special.

Retain your clients

As we've seen, finding clients is expensive and time-consuming, so it's wise to hang on to the clients you have. Customer retention is a big concept in the business world, because everyone knows that it's less costly to keep existing clients than it is to find new ones. So before you have a tantrum and sack a pesky client, remember that it may be better to stop, take a few deep breaths and then give them a call to talk over the problem (see Part 3 for more on managing clients).

Keep in touch to retain clients

Provided you still have something to offer clients you've worked with, give them gentle reminders that you exist. If you're connected to clients with tools like Twitter and LinkedIn, then something as simple as a status update can be enough to remind people that you're alive.

> remind people that you're alive

If you have a few regular clients who keep you well furnished with work, show them you value their work by being friendly. Schedule a meeting (perhaps once a year) to catch up – even if there's no work to discuss. Informal meetings give you both a chance to chat about your wider business issues and your personal lives. By staying at the forefront of a client's mind you improve your chances of being referred and reused.

Offer rewards to your preferred clients

Let your best clients know that you value them, and encourage them to use you again with discounts or exclusive offers.

Understand and meet your client's changing needs

Every job you do will be a learning experience. Often, you'll gain insights into your clients and what they want from you. So make sure you recognise these lessons and adjust your services accordingly. Give your clients what they want and show them you are tuned in to their requirements. If you really want to know what your clients want, ask them. The next time you see them, ask them if they're happy with your service or if there's anything they would like done differently.

Be prepared to act on the feedback you receive. If several of your clients want better payment terms, a faster service or more regular contact, consider giving it to them. If you want to keep them as clients, you may need to adapt to meet their needs. No doubt there are plenty of other freelancers who will happily take your place.

> be prepared to act on the feedback you receive

Tips for making your clients feel valued

New clients are exciting – full of potential, free of problems – but if you can make your existing clients feel just as valued as your sexy new clients, then you'll do well. If your clients feel taken for granted, they may be tempted by another freelancer, especially if the interloper seduces them with attractive rates or an irresistible proposal.

Offer preferential treatment

Put your existing clients ahead of the pack. Let them jump the job queue – and make sure they know it! Work especially hard to meet their deadlines, or accommodate a change to the requested work without additional charges. When you do a favour for a client, make sure they know about it; you could easily bust a gut without your client even noticing.

Offer better terms

Let your trusted, valued clients take a bit longer to pay. You know you can rely on them.

Delay price hikes

Your existing clients won't be too thrilled when you put your prices up. Sugar the pill by giving them an extension on your old rates – but make sure they realise that they're one of a select group of valued clients entitled to this special offer.

 brilliant recap

- Clients can be hard to please, but most days you'll be able to keep them happy.
- The clients you delight are the clients who'll recommend you.
- Incentivise referrals to encourage more of them.
- Improve your chances of landing jobs by being quick off the mark. Clients love attentive, responsive freelancers.
- Finding clients is costly, so value the clients you already have.
- Retain clients by making them feel valued.

Recommended reading

- **http://sethgodin.typepad.com**
- **www.ducttapemarketing.com/blog**
- **www.toprankblog.com**

PART 3

Manage your clients (before they manage you)

Dealing with people is probably the biggest problem you face, especially if you are in business. Dale Carnegie

Clients are the freelancers' lifeblood, but they can be unruly and difficult to please. As we discussed in Part 2, the desired outcome of every piece of work is total customer delight. But the reality is that delight is sometimes impossible to achieve – and on those occasions you're better off just getting the job done. Improve your chances of having happy clients by managing them – manage their projects and manage their expectations. By taking control, you can ensure that your clients are happy, work gets done and you get paid.

CHAPTER 13

Managing clients

Your client is hot for you. They want your stuff. You want to give it to them. Should be simple, right? Alas, you and your client are very different people. Your perceptions vary, you have different frames of references, and one of you is just a bit weird. Because we're all different, it's essential that you *understand* your client's expectations and *manage* those expectations. Rather than let a project drift on, the client patiently waiting for a delivery of apples while you're busy growing bananas, take a few steps to avoid disappointment and disputes.

Explain every detail in the quote

Your proposals and quotes should give the client a firm understanding of what you will do. Document the details:

- Who will do what, and when?
- Who will pay for travel expenses?
- Who will pay for other project costs – do they come out of your budget, or theirs?
- Will you be waiting on the client to provide materials or resources?
- How will you know when the project is complete?
- Is the project divided into milestones?
- Exactly what will your client receive – and in what format?
- How many copies will your client receive?

- How many times will you meet your client?
- How many days will you work in their office?
- How much support will you provide?
- How many times will you update their software?
- Where and when does your involvement end?

Keep in touch

Clients who see work before it's finished are less likely to be disappointed with the end result. Get your client to approve a sample of your work or a mock-up of a design before you really get stuck in. Let them review your work at stages and talk them through your process. Invite questions from your client and be open to suggestions.

You may find it hard to hear a client doubting your work, or saying they don't like something, but criticism and feedback is a big part of freelancing. In time you'll become very good at divorcing yourself from your work, just enough so you can receive feedback calmly and objectively. Listen carefully to your client's views.

> listen carefully to your client's views

Sometimes your clients will make strange requests – asking for things you know to be bad or actively damaging to their business objectives. You'll hear things like 'Could you make the logo bigger?' or 'Maybe we could replace the home page with an animated cabbage?' and all kinds of things that you need to steer the client away from. Never scoff at your clients' requests – but when their ideas are bad, mad or dangerous, politely explain *why*. Your clients aren't experts – they're paying you to be the expert, so if you can support your argument with solid reasoning, you may persuade them. Always leave the choice in their hands, but give them clear reasons for preferring your method.

Dealing with perfectionists

Occasionally you'll encounter *perfectionists* – clients who have unreasonable, unachievable expectations. No matter how amazing your work is, your client will feel you've failed. Your client will want something bigger, better, faster – or something they can't really define. If your client doesn't like what you're doing, you need to establish what they *do* like. Sketch out an alternative, look for examples online or browse your portfolio with the client. Don't let them focus on what they don't like, but get them to point out the things they *do* like.

Once you've agreed on what you're aiming for, do a small piece of work and explain to your client how your work relates to the good examples they've pointed out. Help them see how you're interpreting their desires with your work. If they balk, go back a step and look for examples of what they like *again*.

True perfectionists can be hard to please – as can the clients who consider themselves adept at the skill you offer. You'll encounter the tree surgeon who did Art GCSE, or the business analyst who writes poems, or the film maker whose girlfriend 'has a knack for choosing colours'. People with a smattering of skills or some kind of latent interest in your profession may well meddle in your work. Your best bet is to delicately explain why your work *works*. Explain the reasoning behind your actions and

> delicately explain why your work *works*

explain why their ideas are ill-advised – this will scare off most meddling clients, but sometimes there's nothing you can do. Sometimes clients insist on things that suck. At times like that, you have to let go, and write off the project as one you will never admit to being involved in.

Customer relationship management

If you manage many clients – often juggling several at once – then consider using a simple customer relationship management (CRM) application. CRM is increasingly popular with freelancers who want to organise their contacts, track interactions, monitor the progress of proposals, and gauge how much work is in the pipeline. Some CRM apps combine project management and billing functions, and some pull in social media updates on your contacts, giving you a current view of their life.

Most CRM programs are web-based and require a monthly subscription. Check out:

● **www.batchblue.com**
● **www.zoho.com**
● **http://capsulecrm.com**

CRM systems require an investment of time. You won't get meaningful data or useful insights from your CRM app unless you update it and organise your client contacts from within it.

Communicate clearly for happy relations

Emails encourage rapid responses. It seems okay to dash off a little note, ping it into the ether and then bash out the next missive. Slap, bam, zip. But, all too often, the emails we send in haste are our undoing. How you communicate counts for a lot – and can mean the difference between clients who are impressed by your clarity and clients who are confused by your compositions. The first rule of good business communication is to know *why* you're communicating and to understand *who* you're communicating to.

You also need a firm grasp of your point. What's your goal? Are you asking someone to do something, or exchanging information, or trying to persuade your reader that your plan is brilliant? And who are you addressing? What are their motivations? What is the appropriate way to approach your reader – will they appreciate formality or friendliness? Can you get straight to the point or will you need to warm them up?

The essentials of good written communication

You can't guarantee that your emails will make sense to the recipient, but you can improve the odds by keeping them short. Humans can only tolerate so much information. After a point your reader reverts to thinking about sex, fashion or sports. So keep your messages short. Put the point centre-

keep your messages short

stage – right where it can't be missed. Make the point quickly – don't leave people waiting or searching for the point.

Emails need to be as long as they need to be. The important thing is that you make your point efficiently and clearly. If you need to make lots of points, then turn them into a bullet-pointed list, or add sub-headings to highlight key areas.

You should always re-read your emails, even if you are writing a short, unimportant message. Little typos can easily render a message meaningless. So take a moment to check every email before you hit Send. And for bigger emails, particularly communications with potential clients, before you've got the job, re-read everything twice and run the spell checker over your message. Don't just check the spelling and the grammar; check that you make complete sense, check that you are responding to every question asked of you, and check that you are offering something that fits their needs. Don't hit Send until you're confident that your email will be well received. Projects are won and lost by email – so when it matters, take care.

Pick up the phone when emails just aren't good enough

Emails are limited in their reach. Sometimes, email is not the best way to communicate, so always ask yourself, before you start writing yet another email, 'Should I call this person instead?' By calling someone you can often avoid a sequence of emails – cutting straight to the answers you both need with minimal fuss.

Emails do have their advantages though – and often it's wise to send an email even if you talk through the key points in person or by phone, because the email gives you an evidence trail. If your client forgets a detail, it will be recorded in their inbox. Should there be a dispute, you'll have an undeniable trail of evidence.

 **brilliant** recap

- Prepare your client so they know what they will receive from you.
- Be specific about who is doing what, and when. Clarify assumptions and deliverables.
- Let your client see and review your work periodically.
- Use customer relationship management (CRM) software to keep up with your clients.
- Perfectionists make the worst clients – and require careful management.
- Communicate clearly to keep your clients happy – and call them if you sense any tension in their emails.

CHAPTER 14

Deal with
(and decline)
difficult clients

No matter how hard you try, or how hard you work, some jobs will run off the rails. Projects get complicated, relations sour and the client will blame you for every problem. Troubles can arise from every quarter, and they can be big, small and medium-sized. You can do everything right and still find yourself deep in the quagmire.

Dealing with conflict

So how do you deal with a client who is angry, upset or frustrated? The best place to start is with a phone call. While client disputes often begin with an email – often the email they send you – it's rarely useful to respond with an email. Emails simplify human contact, so they're not always the best way to resolve disputes. With emails, it's all

> don't respond to an angry email with an angry email

too easy to get the wrong idea and to react to something that was never intended. Emails also make it dangerously easy to be rude and angry. Don't respond to an angry email with an angry email.

When an angry email lands in your inbox, read it two or three times before you do anything else. Try to understand your client's view. Why are they reacting like this? Are they really reacting to you, or are they just having a bad day? If you suspect that your client is just in a bad mood, ignore the email for a day. Talk to a friend, colleague or your family about the incident. You may not get any revelations by talking about it, but you will diffuse the sense of conflict within your own body, and you'll make the problem feel smaller. It's often worth sleeping on problems – even if it just gives the client a chance to calm down. Many of my own client conflicts have dissolved overnight.

Try to find a solution to your client's concerns. If they hate something you've done, or are angry about a detail of your arrangement, or disagree with something you've said, try to find a compromise. How can you both get what you want?

It's easy to take criticism personally, and let your ego interfere with negotiations – but this never helps. Monitor your own reactions. Are you being objective? Are you listening carefully to your client's views?

Now pick up the phone. Call your client with a spirit of cooperation and conciliation. Start the conversation with the usual niceties – talk about how you flew a kite or unblocked a drain at the weekend. Offer a solution, or an alternative approach. Let them know you've understood their views and thought hard about a mutually beneficial solution. Be friendly, and *smile*.

offer a solution, or an alternative approach

Remember that you and your client are still friends and the project is still alive. Most clients will appreciate your tact and your generosity, and they may accept your offers. Some clients will remain angry or get fixated on attributing blame. Deflect discussions about blame, because they're fruitless. Side-step any recriminations and nudge your client towards resolutions. Say, 'Yes, I'm sorry you're unhappy about that. But I've been thinking about the best resolution and I'd like to propose that we …'.

If your client is still frothing at the mouth, suggest you meet in person. When you are together you can look at your work or go over details more easily. Be prepared to make concessions. Try to meet your client halfway. But if you haven't done anything wrong, don't accept blame. If the project can't be rescued then your client may use your admission of guilt as an excuse to withhold payment. Focus on a positive outcome, but brace yourself for the worst. Accept that the client may be impossible to please, and you may need to find a way out. If a client wants to remove you from the project, the fairest outcome is that you get paid for the work you have done. They may not like the work you've done, but because they won't give you a chance to rectify it, they should (in fairness) pay you for your time.

At times like this, it's always great if you have a contract in place, but even if there is no written contract, a contract exists between you and the client because contracts are implicitly formed by the agreement you made in person, by email or over the phone. See Part 5 for more on contracts.

Let's remember ...

Big disputes are rare. Minor irritations and disagreements are fairly common, but with a bit of gentle client management you'll be able to get back on track.

When projects can't be saved

If you've exhausted all the obvious options, but you and your client can't reach agreement, then you may need external help. Before you rush off to the small claims court, consider seeking a mediator. Business Link provides lots of information about your next steps, and helps you decide if suing is the best option:

- **www.hmcourts-service.gov.uk**
- **www.businesslink.gov.uk**

How (and when) to say no to clients

Your customers are just like you – they're fallible humanoids with foibles, idiosyncrasies and peccadilloes. So while you may have been raised on the mantra 'The customer is always right', the reality is that the customer may be dangerously wrong. Sometimes you have to save your clients from their own hands, averting disaster by refusing to oblige. Sometimes, you'll want to say no. You may need to refuse a client's bad suggestion or a request to meet an unreasonable deadline. Saying no can be very good for you – it's healthy to show clients that you're not their servant and to remind them that you have other clients to look after.

Be firm, but polite

Offer reasons for your refusal and help your client understand your reasoning. For example, if you're refusing to meet a rush deadline because you're concerned about the quality of your output under such a tight deadline, then the client may be prepared to wait longer for better results.

Offer an alternative

Sweeten the disappointment by offering something in return. Don't let attention linger on the negative – move the focus swiftly on to something positive: for example, 'Sorry, but I can't meet that deadline. *However*, because you're one of my preferred clients I can move aside another client's work and get this done by next week.'

Raise your rates

If a client is pushing you to do something you'd rather not do – like work all night or do something tedious that's beyond your remit – you can deter them with special rates. Special rates, or rush rates, can be invoked whenever you feel like it. Explain to the client that yes, you will work all weekend on their arduous project, but only if they pay your rush rate.

Say you need to think about it

Buy yourself a little time and breathing space. Think over their offer, and consider the value of the work. By creating a pause, you let the client know there's a chance you will say no. If they're smart, they'll start planning alternative solutions in case you say no. Before you make a decision, they may come back with a more favourable offer. And if you do eventually say no, they won't be entirely surprised because you've primed them.

Pre-empt requests you can't accommodate

If you don't want a client to dump an unwieldy project on you at short notice, make sure they know you're really busy. Drop clues into the conversation (e.g. 'I've never been so busy!') so if they do ask, they already know you may well say no.

The danger of saying no

Saying no is hard – in part because it comes with a real risk of losing the client. The harsh reality is that saying no *can* cost you a client – a client who may never come back. If you need to say no, carefully weigh the potential risks with the benefits. Sometimes you'll be glad to risk losing a client if it means keeping your integrity, sanity and bank balance in good health. Clients come and clients go – be prepared to lose a few along the way, because no matter how hard you try, some clients will stray into another freelancer's arms. And when that happens, don't feel bad – it's all part of the rich life of a freelancer.

> saying no *can* cost you a client

 **brilliant** recap

- Despite your best efforts, you will eventually have a disagreement with a client.

- Don't leap to your own defence, but listen carefully to your client's complaint. Try to understand their point of view.

- Let incendiary emails burn themselves out. Don't rush to respond to angry messages from a client.

- Call your client to discuss the issue. Suggest you meet in person. Don't let arguments escalate by email, because you won't get anywhere.

- If you can't resolve the dispute, consider seeking a mediator.

- Sometimes it's good to say no – but be wary as it could cost you the client.

CHAPTER 15

The client's side of the story

M ost of your clients will be great people. Your clients will be driven to do great work, and they'll see your input as instrumental to their greater goals. Your clients will value you, trust you, thank you, recommend you and pay you. Your clients will make freelance life worthwhile. Your clients will bring you interesting projects, teasing your skills in new directions, exposing you to new ideas and new experiences. So while a small minority of your clients will have some strange ideas, the majority will be a joy to work with.

Instead of assuming what clients want from us freelancers, I spoke to a few good clients. The quotes that follow are what they had to say (followed by my interpretation of their words).

Alex Cowell

Alex Cowell is the MD of Cubeworks, one of Brighton's finest digital agencies. They create websites and applications for the public sector as well as for business clients, and often use freelance writers, designers and coders to complement their in-house teams.

 'We like freelancers who put time and thought into their communications.'

If you don't put much effort into your emails or proposals, your client will think you aren't bothered about keeping them as a client. A lack of effort suggests a lack of care. If you can't care enough to think about your communications, don't expect your clients to care enough to hire you again.

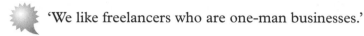

'We like freelancers who are one-man businesses.'

A freelancer who is as organised and professional as a small business is attractive to potential clients. Being business-like makes you easier to deal with. You'll be easier to get hold of, easier to work with and easier to pay.

'We need to be able to trust freelancers around our clients.'

Your clients will take risks with you. In many cases they'll also let you dangerously close to their own clients, taking you along to meetings as part of their company. Whether your freelance status is known or not, you're still acting as a representative of your client. If you are flaky, rude or unhelpful then you make your client look bad. Your client has enough to deal with without worrying about how you might screw up their business relationships.

'We want freelancers to be the expert – and tell us what they need.'

You know what you need to do your job; your client may not be so sure. Be prepared to act as the expert professional, and tell your client how you want to work, and what you need to get your job done. Don't sit back and force your client to do all the thinking.

'We go back to the freelancers who offer solutions instead of problems.'

You will encounter problems. Everyone does. But how you deal with problems is what sets you apart. Instead of running to your client the second a problem arises, take a few minutes to sketch out a solution. Then explain the problem *and* your solution to your client. Your clients want to pay you for doing jobs, and if you can do those jobs without troubling them with petty problems, they'll love you.

Maxine Sheppard

Maxine is the editor of vtravelled – Virgin Atlantic's social travel website. Finding travel writers who can bring travel destinations alive with pulsating prose is no easy task.

'We use freelancers because we don't have the resources in house. By using freelancers we can hire the very best specialist for every job.'

It's obvious, but worth repeating. Your clients want you because you're great at what you do. Your clients have a real need for your specialist skills; you're not there to keep a chair warm.

'We seek out specialists by looking online. People who are not online are unlikely to be picked.'

If all your peers have websites that showcase their wares, is any client likely to pick a freelancer who has nothing online? Clients like freelancers with websites because it gives them a window into the person they want to hire. Websites are enormously communicative. Without a website (or a fulsome LinkedIn profile), you're anonymous, suffocating in a digital vacuum. And clients want reliable professionalism, not mystery.

'Faced with a choice between a freelancer who is on Twitter, and one who is not, we'll pick the one who's on Twitter.'

Your social networks are valuable, and many clients will see that value. They know that your audience – your followers, friends and fans – add to your intrinsic value; particularly for content creators who are likely to share their articles, pictures or videos with people in their online groups. This is free publicity for the client.

 'Freelancers with a network are great too – they can put us in touch with other experts.'

By using freelancers, clients are potentially tapping a much deeper resource by gaining access to all of your contacts – be they other businesses or other freelancers with specialist skills. So remember that your network is not just valuable to you. Many clients will perceive the higher value of a freelancer who is well connected, and may hire with this in mind.

 'We like freelancers who get our brand and pitch work that is clearly suited to our website.'

Clients give clues about what they want. Ignore these at your peril. If you want to skip ahead of the other freelance wannabes, simply take the time to understand your client's brand, their objectives, their audiences and their needs.

 'Freelancers get one chance to impress us.'

If your first contact with your client shows a lack of understanding or a lack of research, don't expect to receive serious consideration the next time you make contact. Make every interaction count, and prove to your client that you care about them enough to do some research.

Darren Fell

As the entrepreneur behind accountancy service Crunch, Darren has been on both sides of the freelance fence, acting as a freelancer and a client. Darren has recruited a wide variety of freelancers to get Crunch up and running, including writers, designers, programmers and screen casters.

'It can be very, very hard to find great freelancers.'

The best freelancers are typically the busiest. The most available, most prominent freelancers are not always the best. Some freelancers are great at self-promotion, but not so great at completing jobs. So remember that clients want you just as much as you want them.

'Ease of contact and communication counts for a lot.'

The freelancer who responds quickly and intelligently to enquiries goes to the head of the class. Far too many freelancers are unreliable and unresponsive, and it's probably the thing that clients least like about taking chances with freelancers. Some of your peers view freelancing as a way to cast aside all responsibility, to take extended holidays and to make a bit of cash in between all-night drinking sessions. Many clients have been burned by unreliable freelancers who go off the radar, miss deadlines and generally flake out at a critical point. By being responsive and professional you can reassure your client and improve your chances of getting repeat work.

'Freelancing doesn't mean you can be any less professional.'

You're outside the corporate bubble, but you're still operating in the wider business environment. As a freelancer, you're independent, but you're still a professional, and you're expected to behave like one. So you're free to choose how you work, but you should still respect your client's time and space.

'Freelancers don't *need* a brand or a logo, but it doesn't hurt.'

Having a visual identity isn't a necessity, but it says a lot to your client. It says you're a serious freelancer, not a chancer. It says you care enough about your work to invest in your marketing. It says you are a professional freelancer.

 'Be fast. Respond to enquiries within minutes.'

Start building what Darren calls 'sales momentum'. Clients love to be attended to. Leave them waiting, and another eager suitor will steal their heart.

Will McInnes

Will McInnes is the managing director and founding partner of successful social media agency Nixon McInnes.

 'We love freelancers who think differently and bring that difference into our space. We enjoy having freelancers around and we get excited by having great people coming to work with us.'

Clients like having you in their company, bringing your own energy, your own specialist skills and your own way of working. For most clients, freelancers bring a refreshing change – provided, of course, that they still get things done.

 'Be nice! We like freelancers who are a pleasure to work with, and who make life easy for us. We want freelancers to demonstrate a willingness to help.'

Not hard, right? Surprisingly, all too many freelancers fail to deliver. Many clients encounter freelancers who are rude, unprofessional and uncooperative, so if you can be reliable, and simply do the work you've promised to do, and be helpful and friendly throughout, you can often leap ahead of other freelancers. Or as Woody Allen said, 'Eighty per cent of success is just showing up.'

'Price isn't the most important thing for us. The price a freelancer puts on themselves tells you lots about how much they value themselves. So we'd never go with the lowest quote.'

Few clients put price above all things. So while it's great to offer value for money, many clients view the cheapest quote as suspect. It's better to price mid-range or at the top of the spectrum.

 'Appearance does matter to us, but it's not about freelancers dressing like estate agents. We just like people to dress like themselves, to feel confident and comfortable in their clothes.'

The days when a suit was the only way to dress for formal occasions are long gone. In many cases, wearing a suit will make you look all wrong. In most cases, try to dress appropriately for your industry – but make sure your clothes reflect who you really are, not who you think you should be.

 'Don't be all things to all people.'

Think about it: if you're building a social media website for a worldwide brand, do you seek out programmers who can build the website, or do you seek a specialist who knows the software inside out? Clearly, when the job is important, you seek a specialist. Will's point is that clients use freelancers because they need short-term specialist knowledge – so what's the point in hiring a generalist when they can find an expert? As we discussed in Part 2, it takes guts to specialise, but if you can specialise in a business area that you enjoy, you and your clients will both enjoy the results.

Recommended reading

- **www.whatmakesthemclick.net**
- **http://clientsfromhell.net** (just for giggles)
- **www.andrewsobel.com/blog**
- *We, Me, Them & It: How to write powerfully for business* by John Simmons (Texere Publishing, 2000)

PART 4

Motivate
yourself and
get stuff done

There is no chance, no destiny, no fate, that can hinder or control the firm resolve of a determined soul.   Ella Wheeler Wilcox

You are the boss. You are now in sole charge of yourself. So when you catch yourself slacking off, or daydreaming, or dawdling, you will have to slap your own wrists and get yourself back to work. For some, the task of motivating and managing one's self is the biggest challenge of being freelance. So, what can you do to keep yourself working hard?

CHAPTER 16

The art of motivation

M otivation means money. Without motivation you can't track down those illusive jobs, you can't get your work done and you can't send invoices. If you can manage your motivation – if you can summon the energy, the force or the will to tackle any challenge – then nothing can stop you.

Define your outstanding tasks

You've got lots on your mind. As well as a vague feeling that you're not doing well enough, you've got a concrete concern that you can't pay this month's rent. Oh, and then there's that difficult client to deal with. And a really tedious proposal to put together. And you know you need to do *something* with your website. And you have a bill to pay, an invoice to amend, a list of clients to call, a dog to walk and your mother wants to talk about Aunt Edna's funeral. You have lots to do, but little motivation for doing it. It's tricky to know what's important, or where to begin. If your mind is bubbling over with competing thoughts and tasks, make sense of it all with a list.

> make sense of it all with a list

Lists are useful. By simply making a list you can transfer the morass of hopes, fears and pending tasks from your mind on to the paper. Once listed, they can be assessed. Once listed, they can be viewed. Once listed, they can be seen for what they are: a humble jumble of *things*. Exorcised from your mind, the things that filled your brain can be sorted, organised and prioritised. Often, the act of listing is enough to calm your mind and give you a clear view of your outstanding tasks.

Now that you've got a list of all your tasks – call it your MegaList if you like – you can begin to see what is important, and what can wait. Only you can decide what your priorities are, but for me my overriding priority is to keep the wheels of commerce rolling along smoothly – so we always have the money we need to survive. So paid work for clients is my first priority. Marketing and administrative tasks come second, because although they might not be critical to my earning today, they are critical to my earning tomorrow. Anything that's not work-related can be dealt with outside work hours. Now, you should be left with a shorter list of work-related tasks to deal with.

Break down your big tasks

It's easy to feel overwhelmed by tasks, especially when the task is not really a task, but an entire project. So if something massive like 'build website' or 'marketing strategy' or 'learn public speaking' are on your to-do list, realise that they're not tasks, but projects that are made up of many smaller tasks. Break these big items down into smaller tasks (or better still, start a new document or spreadsheet for these projects and give them the space they deserve). For example, 'build website' becomes:

- Build website:
  - ask Tom to recommend a web host
  - research open-source website software (WordPress/ Drupal)
  - sketch rough layout of website
  - plan content
  - and so on …

Now all your tasks are in one place, with bigger tasks split into manageable chunks, you can see where to start.

Remember why it's important

Motivation comes from many sources. For you, it may be enough to simply remember why your goal is your goal – that is, *why* is this goal important to you? If 'call potential clients' is one of the most important items on your to-do list, *why* is it important? Clearly, you want to call potential clients because you want their business – and you want work because you want to survive, pay your mortgage, feed your kids and clothe your pets.

Having identified your most pressing task and reflected on why it's important, you should be ready to get started. But wait! If you want to amplify your inner fire, read on.

brilliant action

What's your motivation?

I want to do _____ because _____.

I want to do _____ because _____.

Inspire yourself

What inspires you? Are you inspired by stories of triumph over adversity, or by a ruby-red sunset? Are you inspired by sports-people leaping and lunging to victory, or by the good deeds of philanthropists? Are you inspired by the power and grace of our animal cousins, or by the profit and drive of entrepreneurs? Colour your world with positivity – inspiring tales and uplifting music – leaving angsty tunes and misery memoirs for another day. Focus on positive messages and good moods. If you have miserable friends who burden you with their

focus on positive
messages and good
moods

problems, day after day, year after year, try to balance their misery with friends who are happy, contented and driven. Surround yourself with success – with positive people, influences and examples – and you will set yourself up for the win. Be today who you want to be tomorrow.

Commit yourself

 'Until one is committed, there is hesitancy, the chance to draw back, always ineffectiveness, concerning all acts of initiative and creation. There is one elementary truth, the ignorance of which kills countless ideas and splendid plans: that the moment one commits oneself, then Providence moves too. All sorts of things occur to help one that would never otherwise have occurred. A whole stream of events issues from the decision.'

Johann Wolfgang von Goethe

Bigger challenges or unappealing tasks demand *commitment*. Until you start, you have the option to back out. You can retreat and retire and pretend it never happened. But once you start, you're *committed*.

Your chances of success increase when you publicly state your aims: do you dare fail when the world is watching? Raise the stakes by publicly declaring your commitment to a goal. Tell people what you're going to achieve. Post a promise on Twitter, Facebook or your blog. Give yourself a deadline. Tell your friends. Commit yourself loudly and boldly. Make success inevitable and failure impossible – or at least really, really embarrassing.

Speak with certainty and positivity

We all like to be right – that's why few people make bold claims or definitive statements. And that's fine if you're talking about the weather:

- 'I *think* it *might* rain today,'

but not so good if you're talking about important goals:

- 'I *think* I *might* look for a job today.'

I've italicised the weak words in these two statements. These weak words are the escape routes that people commonly drop into their speech. These might seem like harmless caveats, but they are sapping words that undermine your motivation, because you tell yourself that you *might* do this, you'll *probably* try to do such and such, and every time you weaken your words you're essentially saying:

- 'I probably *won't* do anything at all. I will probably continue to talk big and act small.'

Instead of building escape routes into your speech, cut them out and commit yourself to your plans. Make definite statements about what you are going to do. Be bold, be certain and be confident:

- 'I will call three new prospects on Tuesday. I really want to work with them, so it's worth the effort.'
- 'I will chase all my outstanding invoices on Thursday, because my cash flow is starting to suffer.'
- 'I'm going to the Chamber of Commerce networking breakfast on Friday, because networking will improve my chances of having a successful freelance career.'

Start with small steps and build momentum

If the vastness of your massive to-do list is causing you to freeze up, too overwhelmed to move, look for an easy, achievable task to get you started. Build momentum by starting with something small. As you complete tasks, you'll feel energised by the satisfaction of getting things done. Reinvigorated, you'll soon be ready to tackle the bigger tasks on your list.

Get help

If you need help to overcome an obstacle, go for coffee with someone and talk it over. Release the problem – get it out of yourself and into the wild. There's a good chance that you'll find a solution, but even if the answer remains elusive, you'll feel better for airing the issue.

Your tasks may be bigger than you and bigger than your skills. Know when you need help, and be comfortable asking for help.

> know when you need help

If you get to know other freelancers you'll have a support network ready to rely on when problems arise. You'll also be able to return the favour, and use your experiences of freelancing to help others. As a global union of freelancers, we're all in it together.

You can also find valuable advice scattered freely around the web. But heed Simon Booth-Lucking's warning and 'Don't read too many productivity blogs' – otherwise your quest for productivity nirvana will lead you to procrastination hell.

Relish every win

You may be more successful than you think. Often, our *attitude* to our achievements is just as important as the actual achievements, because while some people revel in their achievements, shouting loudly about the good things, others play them down, excusing themselves from the glory with a disclaimer or a caveat, saying things like 'Anyone would have done the same – in fact most people would have done better!'

Think back over the past few days and weeks. What have you done to be proud of? Are you researching a new way of life – or have you boldly quit your job to go freelance? Or have you been freelance for a while, earning your own income through the application of your own skills? Before you write off these achievements as being ordinary or sub-par, remember that you are doing something daring – something lots of people would love to try. So wherever you stand in your freelance journey, acknowledge that you're doing something challenging – something with no guarantees of success. Make a list of your achievements so far and remember the steps you took to get there. Realise the power of your accomplishments and be proud.

> acknowledge that you're doing something challenging

Focus on the positive, neglect the negative

Even the most fulfilled, motivated people get things wrong. It's inevitable that some things won't work out the way you hoped. You'll forget something, miss a deadline, annoy a client or lose a job. And that's all cool. The trick is to reflect on failures and accept them, but then move on. Remember that once a failure has occurred, there's no way to undo it. Accept the things you can't change and focus on the things you can change. Don't focus on failures. Spend more time looking at your successes – because they will suggest the path to future successes and fill your mind with happiness.

'Rolling in the muck is not the best way of getting clean.'

Aldous Huxley

Accept setbacks, lulls and outright catastrophes

Big challenges often bring *risks*. In trying to do something great, you're always going to invite the threat of setbacks. Opening up to failure is a good sign – it's healthy. The alternative is to shut yourself indoors where nothing can go wrong, but consequently nothing can go right either. Accept that, as you make your way into freelancing, you will experience some failures, some setbacks and some sadness. No freelance career was ever created without a few hiccups, so don't expect too much from yourself. Give yourself a break!

 'Don't set your expectations too high – otherwise it will be impossible to get started.'

Simon Booth-Lucking

Keep your eyes fixed on the horizon

As you progress down the long, winding path to freelance enlightenment, it's easy to get muddled up in the details of your days. Before you get too confused, reconnect with your main objectives – what are you doing all this for? Is every effort leading you closer to your goals? Remember why your primary objective is important to you, and then cut back on anything that wastes your time, or doesn't help you get closer to your goals.

Tackle the bigger issues

Your tasks and goals can be affected by other problems or unresolved issues. Perhaps the real reason you avoid networking is your anxiety around new people. Or maybe you lack motivation because you're depressed. Or maybe you can't sit still and work because your bad back gives you headaches when you sit. Or maybe you can't concentrate because you're worried about a family member, or because your relationship is breaking down. If you are beset by problems beyond your work, think about how you can deal with them. Freelancing is tough enough without personal stresses clouding your mind.

brilliant recap

- You're the boss now and you have to manage your own workload and your own motivation.

- Unmotivated freelancers don't find work and they don't complete jobs – so there's a huge value to remaining motivated.

- Define what you need to do: write a list.

- Remember how your tasks contribute to your bigger goals, and why those are important to you.

- Inspire yourself with positive messages.

- Commit yourself to your goals – tell the world!

- Congratulate yourself for every victory.

CHAPTER 17

Choose a productive place to work

One of the most wonderful things about being freelance is that you have the freedom to work anywhere. I've worked on the beach, at home, from my client's offices and in a multitude of pubs, cafés and restaurants. I've worked on trains, planes and automobiles. I've worked at home in my pants, on the beach in my swimming trunks and once, when I was a bit poorly, I wrote some copy in my pyjamas.

Work from home

The home office makes a great deal of sense: it's free, it's available and it's comfortable. As a new freelancer you'll want to minimise expenditure, so if your home is available, try using it as an office.

Make your home office usable as an office

You don't need a spare room to work from home. You just need to find a little space where you can work undisturbed. A kitchen table or the corner of a bedroom may be enough to get you started. Create a space which, although it doubles up as your dining room or your laundry hamper, can accommodate you and your work without hindering your progress. Try to get away from distractions like TVs, chores and your family.

✖ **brilliant** dos and don'ts

When you work from home:

Do

- ✔ Define your working hours – and stick to them.
- ✔ Call people when you can – the human contact will keep you sane.
- ✔ Talk to the people you live with about what you're doing. You'll need their support.
- ✔ Get out – entire days can whizz past without you leaving the house or speaking to people.
- ✔ Make it fun – you're free!

Don't

- ✖ Let your work seep into your home life.
- ✖ Delay your work in favour of household chores.
- ✖ Forget why you're at home (to work).
- ✖ Get too relaxed – start every day as though you're going to visit the biggest or best client you've ever had.
- ✖ Let your friends or family lead you astray – you may need to remind them you have work to do.

The trouble with working from home

The biggest problem of working from home is the isolation. Entire days can pass without human contact. The next time you see someone, you'll hardly know how to have a conversation. Freelancers need to be easy and effective communicators, so if working from home means you rarely see people, and become a less confident and less effective communicator, look for an office.

brilliant tip

Want to work from home, but lack the space to do it properly? Why not join the roster of people working out of their sheds? See **www.shedworking.co.uk** for the latest shedworking developments.

Work from an office – or cowork

All around you are under-populated offices. A desk here, a room there – many businesses offer these desk spaces to micro-businesses and freelancers. So if working from home doesn't suit you, look for local businesses advertising desk space. You can get a professional environment, with all the utilities and facilities taken care of, for a fraction of the price of hiring your own office. Look for 'desk space' or 'desk available' adverts in your local press.

Coworking

Nothing to do with cows, coworking offers freelancers the perks of company life without the drawbacks. In coworking spaces, people come together to work on their own projects. So in one space you have many people working independently, but harmoniously. United by their modest needs for heat, light, power, internet and coffee, freelancers first came together in the US, creating rough-and-ready offices as an alternative to working from coffee houses and bed-

coworking has quickly grown into a global trend

rooms. Coworking has quickly grown into a global trend, with shared spaces popping up around the world. The UK has co-working spaces in cities including Birmingham, Bournemouth, Brighton, Bristol, Leeds, Lewes, London, Manchester, Milton Keynes and Sheffield.

Coworking spaces are designed to accommodate freelancers with small budgets and a need for flexibility. Traditional offices are often prohibitive because they come with high rents that you must pay for 6–12 months. Coworkers prefer to pay-as-they-go, using only as much space as they need. Your coworking office may be a little scruffier than a traditional office, but if you're paying 50 per cent less rent, then you can probably tolerate chairs that don't match the carpets.

Use Google to find spaces near you, or try the official coworking wiki: **http://coworking.pbworks.com**

The joy of coworking

Coworking spaces are full of smart people doing interesting stuff. Coworkers make a deliberate choice to work with *people*. So the people you meet in coworking offices will be welcoming and friendly. In no time at all you can expect to make friends and start developing a new community of colleagues. Just because you haven't got a regular job, doesn't mean you can't swap biscuits, gossip and ideas with new people. And the secret bonus to coworking is that it's discreet, incidental *marketing*. By simply being visible, by working in a shared space, you increase your chances of finding work. By coworking with other professionals you can quietly demonstrate your professionalism and reliability – so you'll be the first person they think of when they need a freelancer like you.

Because coworking spaces often house independent and nomadic workers, there is a genuine thirst for socialising – so expect to find plenty of parties, picnics and pub visits.

If you try coworking, go with an open mind and a smile on your face. Say hello to the people you meet. Be sociable. Your coworkers will not always come to you – you need to make a little effort. But if you do, you will soon get to know the regulars. Coworking has been instrumental in my own freelance fortunes.

you need to make a little effort

I'm something of a serial coworker, having worked from The Werks, West Werks, The Skiff and Chapel Studios in Brighton and Hove; and The Trampery, Hub Islington and TechHub in London. Coworking is a great way to meet people and to kick-start your freelance career – so look for spaces near you.

Work with friends

If your friends are toiling alone at home, why not work together? You get companionship and a comfortable working environment for free! No rent, no contract and you can motivate each other to work harder.

Work abroad

As a freelancer, you can do what you like. As long as you can communicate with clients and get work done, you can work wherever, whenever. Want to work from the beach? You can. Want to spend six months sipping cocktails in Thailand, tapping out some code while the sun goes down? You can. Want to live in Berlin for six months? You can. Want to do all your work in a purple babygrow, while hopping along a treadmill? You can. You *shouldn't*, but you can.

While some freelance jobs require your physical presence, many others do not. Thanks to high-speed internet connections, we can Skype and video-chat our way to effective communications. We can collaborate and communicate wherever we are. So providing your clients trust you (and you repay their trust) then you can wander the earth.

 recap

● You can work from anywhere: choose a place that makes you happy and helps you focus on your work.

● Your home is probably the best place to get started.

● If you work from home, try to create boundaries between your home and office life.

● Coworking is affordable office space that's perfect for freelancers.

CHAPTER 18

Healthy body, healthy mind

Freelancing is hard work. If ordinary employment is like running your car on Britain's well-maintained roads, going freelance is like entering the Paris–Dakar rally; it's great fun, but you're going to endure more stress and strain than usual. Freelancing amplifies life's highs and lows. Yes, you will be more stressed at times. Yes, you will fret about money. Yes, you will miss your holiday allowance and the security of sick pay. Yes, yes, yes. But then there are the highs – those glorious highs! Like the joy when you win a prized contract or the delight when things go *right*. Things that go right because of the choices you made, because of the career you engineered! The satisfaction of feeding yourself and your loved ones with provisions purchased with the money you earned – *the money people paid you for the work you did*. From inception to completion, it's all *you* – and that will make you happy. You'll be happy too because you're free to express your own vision of work, play and life itself.

So you're in a good spot. Make sure you stay there by taking good care of your most valuable assets – your mind and body. You're selling *you*, so look after your product.

Healthy body

Health is a precious commodity. Your work and your income depend entirely on you, so the importance of remaining healthy is impossible to ignore. Minimise minor illnesses by eating, sleeping and exercising well. Invest a little bit of time in the health of your own organism, or risk physical and mental breakdown and, eventually, financial ruin. By focusing on prevention you may side-step minor health irritations and remain productive.

Eat well

You get out what you put in, so if you want a calm, efficient body that can fight illness, don't stuff your face with chips and doughnuts. It might sound obvious, but going freelance is a good time to review your eating habits, because if you get sick you don't have the luxury of recuperating on the sofa watching Jeremy Kyle at your employer's expense. Don't turn into a health freak and adopt a diet of nettles and lint, but temper your cake habit with a daily apple, or have a glass of water in between beers. Do whatever feels right for you, but recognise the direct link between your diet, your health, and your fortunes.

> temper your cake habit with a daily apple

Exercise well

Your body wasn't built for office life. Sitting down all day is unnatural, and your body doesn't like it much. If your work is sedentary, make up for it by filling your free time with movement. Run, walk, ride. Just do *something*.

Just move

If you're stressed, lethargic or depressed, go for a run. Hop on a bike. Take a dip in the pool. Obviously, if you have health problems or back pain you should ask your doctor what kinds of exercise are safe for you. Good exercise is safe and pain-free.

brilliant tip

Make exercise easy and inevitable. Incorporate exercise into your daily routine by cycling to work, using more public transport, taking the stairs, joining sports clubs or playing physical games with your kids.

Sleep well

If you work all night to meet a deadline, don't expect to be ready for work the next morning. Clearly, the best plan is to avoid the late nights in the office in the first place, because it's highly unlikely that the quality or quantity of your production is going to be optimal at 4:00 in the morning. If an all-nighter is unavoidable, then give yourself a break the next day: sleep late, finish early then get back to a normal sleep pattern. There are only 24 hours in a day, and any attempt to extract more time from those finite hours is doomed to failure.

Work well

The days of a freelancer bulge at the sides. In between marketing, responding to enquiries, managing clients, taking calls and updating your accounts, you'll have to squeeze in a little bit of *work*. The temptation is to pack out each day like an overstuffed suitcase, with an errant sock poking out the side. Beware the temptation to work flat-out for days at a time. Without breaks, *you* will break. Stop for a cup of tea, a chat with a co-worker or a walk around the block. Do anything that gives you a change of scene and your body a change of position. Try to get your blood moving a bit. Read a book, ride your bike, fly a kite – but don't let yourself stay hunched over your laptop for hours on end.

Ergonomics

The way we work, the physical positions we put ourselves in, can cause all kinds of problems. Hunching over a laptop, gripping a vibrating tool or simply sitting on a chair that's too low, too high or too soft can all lead to injuries. You may think you feel fine and that your body is happy with the way you work, but that's how it happens; you cruise along, merrily oblivious to the strain your body is tolerating, until it breaks. By the time you realise something's wrong,

> by the time you realise something's wrong, it's too late

it's too late. Repetitive strain injuries (RSI) and the problems induced by poor working practices can cause acute pain and may stop you working. Prevent significant loss of earnings by treating your body with care and avoiding breakdowns.

How are you working? Do you sit comfortably, with your monitor at a good height? Do you use a mouse that won't induce carpal tunnel syndrome? Are you wearing the right gloves to dampen the vibrations, or taking the appropriate number of breaks? If you're not sure, ask your peers. How do they protect themselves from injury?

brilliant tip

Repetitive strain injuries (RSI) lay low many good freelancers. Whether you're typing or carpeting, take steps to prevent RSI because once you've got it, you've got it. Search online for exercises you can do to prevent RSI or seek the advice of a physiotherapist.

Happy holidays

Okay, time to fess up. There is one major perk to having a 9–5 job that is hard to beat: *the holiday allowance*. As a permanent employee you get 20 days to use as you please. You can use them whenever you like and there's absolutely no penalty for using them all up. They're yours, and you get paid the same amount every month, even though you spent half the month sunning your butt on a Bermudan beach. Only when you give up your holiday allowance do you realise just how amazing it is. Free holiday! Those days are gone.

 'Every man who possibly can should force himself to a holiday of a full month in a year, whether he feels like taking it or not.'

William James

As a freelancer, holidays feel very different. First, you're *not* paid for your holiday time, and second your break is likely to have repercussions – clients might need a job completed, an opportunity might arise – and there will be little or nothing you can do about it. Oh, and because it's a holiday you'll be haemorrhaging money all over the place. It's a triple-whammy. And holidays are harder to take because you care about what happens when you're away – you care because your business is your life! If problems flare up during your holiday, you'll find them hard to ignore. And if you remain out of reach, you might be saved the stress but your relaxing holiday could come at the expense of a client, a job or your reputation. So, who's ready for a holiday?

> you care because your business is your life

brilliant tip

Book a holiday. Do it now. Decide when to take a break, put it in your diary and start telling your clients. As the holiday approaches, remind your clients that you're going away. Let them know how contactable you will be (if at all) and when you will be back. But book the holiday, otherwise it may never happen.

Take a break

Although holidays are harder to take when you're freelance, they are still essential. Holidays can be cheap, short and simple – the important thing is that you take a break from your work and do something different. You don't need to leave the country. You don't even need to leave your home. You just need a break from your daily routine.

brilliant dos and don'ts

Do

✔ Take a proper break at least once a year. Refresh your brain. Get away from it all.

✔ Tell your clients that you're going away.

✔ Accept that you might lose out on some work while you're away.

✔ Fill your mind with your holiday and forget about work – if only for a few days.

✔ Have a way to keep in touch with your work – if only so you can respond to enquiries.

✔ Take smaller breaks during the year.

Don't

✗ Rearrange your holiday at the last minute because of a job offer.

✗ Spend your entire holiday checking emails and doing small favours for your clients.

✗ Think about work constantly – it will all be there when you get back.

✗ Expect to work every day for years on end – you'll work yourself into an early grave.

✗ Feel bad about taking holidays. Your clients won't think twice before booking their two weeks in Malaga. Everyone is entitled to holidays, and taking breaks will make you a better freelancer.

Healthy mind

Freelancing is tough. You'll worry, fret and struggle over big challenges, and you'll deal with them on your own, in your own way. Yes, you'll have the support of friends and freelancers (as long as you look for it) but the ultimate responsibility for your success or failure rests with you. And sometimes that can feel like a lot of pressure – especially if other things depend on your success as a freelancer – things like feeding your children and paying your mortgage.

Stress and anxiety are normal parts of life. A life without stress is a life without challenge. The important thing is that you have a way to release your stress. If stress piles upon stress, churning around in your body and mind, you'll find it hard to focus. Without a way to release stress you may find it hard to focus on your work.

> a life without stress is a life without challenge

brilliant dos and don'ts

Do

✔ Exercise to release stress.

✔ Talk to people about your worries and any problems you face with your work.

✔ Be honest when times are bad.

✔ Accept a degree of stress and anxiety in your life – it's totally normal!

✔ Boost your confidence by pushing yourself to face up to challenges.

✔ Take a break if you're feeling stressed.

Don't

✘ Drink too much coffee.

✘ Pretend things are fine when they're not.

✘ Rely on booze to relax.

✘ Work all night and expect to feel good the next day.

✘ Rely on drugs for confidence or happiness.

✘ Expect to never feel nervous.

Get support

The problems you'll face as a freelancer are universal. If you've encountered a problem that no other freelancer has ever faced, well done – that's quite an achievement. So rather than fret over a problem alone, seek help from another freelancer – or just talk it over with your partner, parent or friend. You don't need to confide in a freelancer to get the benefit; sharing your concerns with a wall might make you feel a little better. Just saying the words out loud and letting them fly free of your body is enough. The ideal scenario is to have friends who freelance, because they will truly understand what you're going through. Which takes us right back to the value of networking.

If you're struggling with the business elements of freelancing, seek help from Business Link, a mentor or a coach.

Income protection insurance

As a freelancer you don't have the safety net of sick pay. So what happens if you're too sick to work? Well, you're on your own. This is another reason why a healthy savings account is always a great idea, but if you're worried about having enough money to cover periods of illness, you could try accident and sickness insurance, which can cover your costs until you get better.

 brilliant recap

- Freelance holidays are not like the holidays you enjoy as a permanent employee.

- While holidays can be stressful and hard to take, you must take a break.

- Book your holiday in advance. Without an actual holiday booked it's all too easy to let work fill the time.

- Explain to your clients how long you'll be gone for, and how contactable you'll be during your holiday.

- It's okay to keep in touch with important clients and projects during your break – providing that's what you (and your family) want.

CHAPTER 19

Healthy computers

The computers are taking over. We're all plugging our minds into the mainframe, becoming cybernetic tele-mutants from the future, guided by GPS, dependent on pokes, nudges and status updates. It's a safe bet that, whatever profession you're in, computers play a part in your work. Even freelance stonemasons will need a computer to maintain their records, find jobs and communicate with clients. So you might not sit in front of a computer all day long, but technology remains a pivotal part of your business, and your computer's health remains critical to the smooth operation of your enterprise.

Computer failures can be costly, embarrassing and potentially disastrous. Imagine having to tell a client that you are going to miss a deadline by three weeks because you've lost all their work (and didn't have a backup). Imagine being unable to work because your laptop breaks and ends up in the shop for a week. What would your clients think of a freelancer so ill-prepared for problems?

> computer failures can be costly

Prepare to fail

Assume the worst. Regardless of how new, shiny or expensive your computer is, assume that today it is going to break. Be prepared for everything to go wrong *right now*. If your hard drive went up in smoke right now, would you be able to access all your files? If your computer succumbed to viruses, how would you continue working on that half-completed project? If your laptop was stolen, how would you get back to work?

Seamless, persistent, automatic back-ups

One wonderful aspect of our web-connected lives is that we no longer need to store our important stuff on disks in our homes or offices, where it can be burnt, stolen, damaged or lost. Today, there is absolutely no need to lose data. Back-ups can be automated so you barely need think of them.

Convenient back-up tools

Dropbox is the king of automatic 'cloud-based' backups. Dropbox gives you a new folder on your desktop, and every file you drop into that folder is automatically backed up – persistently and consistently. If you use more than one computer, you can connect them all to your one Dropbox account, so wherever you work, your files will all be the same, and constantly synchronised between all connected computers. Dropbox also provides a web interface to your stored files, so if you need to work from a strange computer one day you can get at your files from any computer with a web connection. 2GB of storage comes free with Dropbox; if you need more space you can pay for it. Alternatives to Dropbox include:

- Windows Live Mesh
- Dmailer
- Syncplicity.

Anti-virus software

Your computer is under attack. Even the most sensible of web users can be exposed to viruses and spyware. And many viruses are clever enough to sail under the radar of your anti-virus software. Keeping free of malware is hard, but anti-virus and anti-spyware software are essential to give your computer (at least) a fighting chance.

brilliant tip

If your computer slows down, or starts behaving oddly, you may be infected. Your computer needs the digital equivalent of chicken soup: a trip to your friendly neighbourhood computer shop. For a reasonable fee you can get viruses removed and have your computer back to maximum performance. If you consider the potential time lost to a computer that is being slowed and confused by a virus, then the cost of getting it fixed is a reasonable investment.

Free anti-virus software

Anti-virus software doesn't need to be expensive. There are many free products out there, including:

- Microsoft Security Essentials
- Avast!
- AVG Free.

Essential apps

Here are a few choice applications to help you get things done.

Time-keeping

You're charging for your time, so you'll probably want to record how much time you spend on each project.

- SlimTimer – simple, elegant and free time-tracking software in your browser.

- Klok – a downloadable app; choose from a simple, free version or pay for the full-time tracking program.

- ManicTime – tracks what you're doing on your computer so you can bill for every hour spent working.

Brain-dumping

Lists are simple but effective for organising your work. Use an app to make the process more interactive.

- Todobedobedo – a free web app that makes it fun to complete tasks.

- EpicWin (iPhone app) – turns your tasks into a game.

- Bubbl.us (for making mind-maps) – a great way to visualise complex ideas and tasks.

Productivity

- ActiveInbox – a Gmail extension that helps you represent emails as tasks, rather than messages.

- Basecamp – manage projects within a system your clients can use too.

- Google Docs – collaborate on documents with your clients.

- Lifehacker's Texter – get keyboard shortcuts for all the things you regularly type – like your email signature, your web domain, your address or your business name.

- Rapportive – a Gmail extension that displays contact information alongside your emails.

 **brilliant** recap

- Your computer is an essential part of your enterprise.
- Have back-up plans just in case your computer erupts in flames.
- There's no excuse for not having current back-ups of your data. Modern software makes backing-up seamless and persistent.
- Use one of the free antivirus programs to protect your machine from malware.
- Explore other apps to improve your productivity and time keeping.

Recommended reading

- **http://lifehacker.com**
- **www.persistenceunlimited.com**
- **www.43folders.com**

PART 5

Protect
yourself:
finances, cash
flow, credit
control and
contracts

A verbal contract isn't worth the paper it's printed on.

Samuel Goldwyn

Being a brilliant freelancer doesn't count for much if you fail to get paid. You can have adoring clients, a bulging portfolio, an enviable market position and a diary packed with projects, but if you don't invoice or collect the cash, then it's all for nothing. Book-keeping and credit control are background activities – they're the uninspiring administrative stuff that every freelancer does, though few talk about. But financial control is highly valuable, and a lack of control can lead you to the brink of collapse. Let's look at steps you can take to keep your finances in order.

CHAPTER 20

How to keep financial records

You must keep records. It's the law. Whether you use a simple spreadsheet or slick software, you must record the money that flows in and out of your business. If you're trading as a limited company then you must produce a set of accounts each year – although you'll probably get an accountant to do this for you.

Spreadsheets

If you operate as a sole trader, a simple spreadsheet may be all you need. Your accountant may have a template you can use, or they may tell you what to record and how to organise your spreadsheet.

Accountants often charge according to how much of the work they have to do – so if you provide them with a set of well-kept books (either as an output from book-keeping software or as spreadsheets) then you'll pay less. If you're a busy freelancer, it can be tempting to favour client work over your book-keeping – especially as client work pays! But don't forget that a little bit of book-keeping soon pays for itself by helping you track your finances.

The benefits of keeping good records

While some freelancers like to hoard receipts and invoices in jumbled boxes and dump them on their accountant's doorstep once a year, if you maintain records as you go, you'll always know:

● how much you've invoiced
● who owes you money
● how much you've spent
● how your income compares to your expenditure (net profit).

These numbers are crucial, particularly when you're short of cash, or wondering why you seem to be incredibly busy but lacking profit. Having easy access to these numbers is often enough to highlight flaws in your approach.

Book-keeping software

You can choose from traditional software that you install on your computer, or choose web-based software and keep your records online. Before you choose a program, ask your accountant if they can work with the software you're considering.

Possibly the greatest benefit of book-keeping software is that invoicing and accounts are integrated. You can use your software to raise a professional-looking invoice and send it to your client, and the relevant accounts are automatically updated. Doing the same with spreadsheets would add a few steps to your process and take considerably longer.

Book-keeping software options are:

● Crunch
● FreeAgent
● Clear Books.

Allowable expenses

Once you've decided *how* to record your transactions, you need to know *what* to record. Your financial transactions fall broadly into two categories: money coming in, and money going out. The jobs you invoice are likely to account for 100 per cent of the money coming into your business, but your expenses will be numerous and varied. It's vital that you understand what expenses can be associated with your business, because when your business doesn't pay, you do.

Your business has many expenses – the costs it incurs during operations – and it's only fair that your business pays these costs. The more expenses your business pays, the less profit it makes and therefore the less tax it pays. So while there's an advantage to putting allowable expenses through your business, there can be severe penalties for anyone who abuses the system.

> there can be severe penalties for anyone who abuses the system

You may be surprised to learn what can be classified as a business expense, but it's worth getting the advice of an accountant because allowable expenses do change and your situation may be different from the norm. Attempting to claim anything that's not a legitimate business expense could lead you into trouble with HMRC.

Business expenses include (but are not limited to):

- **Office rent** – even if you work from home you may be able to claim a percentage of your rent or mortgage cost as a business expense.

- **Travel expenses** – trains, taxis, flights and parking can all be claimed back if you are travelling to a necessary business meeting.

- **Equipment and materials** – you can claim back things like stationery, computer peripherals and any consumables you use in your work.

- **Telephone and broadband** – you may need to separate any personal use from your phone and internet connection costs.

- **Bicycle expenses** – if you buy a bike primarily for work use (at least 50 per cent work use) then you can buy it through your company. You can also claim a set amount for the mileage you do on your bike.

- **Mileage** – keep track of the miles you drive and cycle for work.

- **Books and magazines** – claim back any professional publications or work-related books.

- **Subsistence** – you can claim back food costs incurred while travelling.

- **Entertaining** – providing you are entertaining for business, you may be able to claim back your costs.

Get professional advice

Your allowable expenses depend on whether you are a sole trader or a limited company, so to make sure you're claiming back every expense you can (and nothing you can't!) get the advice of an accountant. An accountant will be able to clarify your questions in minutes, and that way you're protected against a knock on the door from an angry HMRC inspector. Indeed, accountants can often pay for themselves in minutes by helping you claim every legitimate expense.

 **brilliant** recap

- Keeping track of your finances doesn't have to be complicated – or expensive.

- Whether you choose a simple spreadsheet or a versatile web application, make sure you know how much you've invoiced, how much you've been paid and how much you've spent.

- Most accountants charge according to the amount of work you make them do. Reduce your accountancy costs by keeping better records.

- Claim all allowable expenses – but don't claim anything that isn't a genuine (and allowable) business expense (e.g. clothing).

CHAPTER 21

Cash flow and the need for credit control

Perhaps the single biggest killer of freelance careers is cash flow, or the lack of it. Even the most frugal freelancer has expenses – things like rent, hosting, materials, software, travel, Choco Leibniz, printing and stationery – so money will always flow easily *out* of your bank account. To compensate for this leakage, you need to make sure that money flows *in* to your bank account, primarily by encouraging your clients to pay you on time. If money doesn't continue flowing into your bank account, you can quickly find yourself unable to meet your expenses and unable to pay yourself.

Get paid (credit control)

Because you let your clients pay you some time after you raise the invoice – such as 7, 14 or 30 days later – you are effectively giving your clients *credit*. Hence the need for credit control.

Your clients are busy people, and your invoice is much less significant to them than it is to you. So don't expect them to receive your invoices with reverence, respond to them immediately and send you a telegram to announce the payment. More likely, they'll just add your invoice to the pile. And then forget all about it.

If you want to get paid on time, and reduce your chances of running into a cash flow crisis, take a few steps to encourage prompt payment.

Choose payment terms that are favourable to you

Big companies might go around offering 30-day credit terms, but can you really afford to? No! Maybe when you're established, and you've been busy enough to reach a stage where you're not eagerly waiting for each invoice to be paid. But in the early days, or when work levels dip, you should constrict your credit terms to better suit your finances. You can offer as much credit as you like – in fact you can offer no credit at all and ask for payment on delivery or payment on receipt of invoice. Try to balance out your need for money with the need to give your clients some flexibility. So try offering your clients 7 or 14 days to pay. Again, many larger companies will only pay your invoice according to their standard terms, which are likely to be 30+ days after invoicing. But many smaller companies *will* accept your own payment terms, providing you discuss them before you start work.

> you can offer as much credit as you like

Explain your payment terms – before you do any work!

Prime your clients for what will happen once the work is done. Don't let them be surprised that you're chasing payment just seven days after invoicing. Most clients will be sympathetic to your needs, because they understand the challenges of cash flow as much as anyone.

Get money before you start work

Ask for a deposit. It's quite normal, and makes perfect sense, especially if you're working for a new client, or starting a project that will take weeks or months to complete. If you wait until the job is finished before you invoice, you could be waiting a long time to get paid. And if you're working for a new client, how do you know they can be trusted? Are you happy to invest your time and energy into their work, knowing nothing about their finances, their history or their personal morals? Even if you trust your clients, asking for a deposit is a great way to balance out your cash flow – it also has a bonus effect of psychologically committing your clients to the project. I've had a few flaky clients who think they can back out of a project or renegotiate the terms in the middle of the job – things that might not have happened if they'd already paid 50 per cent.

Chase early, chase often

There is no shame in asking for the money that is owed to you. When you chase payment for an invoice, you are not asking for money personally, you are working for your business, collecting money that is owed to your business. So don't think of it as a personal matter. If your invoice is one day overdue, you are absolutely entitled to chase for payment. Don't be bad-humoured about it, but do give your client a call. Remain friendly but firm. Know your rights. Don't accept any nonsense – there's no excuse for not being paid.

know your rights

Beware not getting paid because your client is not getting paid

There is a common scenario in the freelance world, and it goes a little something like this: you, as a freelancer, build a website for MegaDigital, a web agency. Their client is Hoxton Spanners. MegaDigital doesn't pay you on time, so you chase them. They claim that because Hoxton Spanners has not paid them, they cannot pay you. By law, this argument does not hold. It is not fair or reasonable to withhold payment for this reason. However, that does not stop some clients from using this as an excuse. And if they do, it can be hard to push them for payment – particularly because your client might genuinely be waiting for money to arrive before they can afford to pay you.

The best way to avoid this scenario is to ask your client if your payment will depend on any outside factors, such as their own payments from clients. Another good way to avoid being screwed in this situation is to get a deposit before you do any work. With 50 per cent up front you're less at risk if your client delays payment.

Invoice correctly (and according to your client's requirements)

Accounts departments are melancholic places, populated by pale faces in dark suits. Their function is to count money and to enter data. Your invoice, that important document that means so much to you and your future, is, in the hands of an accounts department, just another bit of data. And if your data is not correctly formatted, according to their rules, it gets rejected. Oh, and if your invoice is rejected for being incomplete, you won't get an email alerting you to this – your invoice will just be added to the leaning 'query' pile.

> your invoice is just another bit of data

Ask your client if they have any special requirements for invoicing. They may insist you quote their purchase order number, or that invoices are posted to a specific address. Get this information *before* you raise an invoice!

Make sure your invoices include:

- invoice date
- due date
- your address
- your company registration number
- your invoice number
- the client's job/project/invoice number
- your VAT number (if you have one)
- your bank account details (if required for electronic payments)

- a clear breakdown of what you are invoicing (number of hours, rate, etc.)
- the client's company name and their full address.

Dealing with clients who won't – or can't – pay

Unless you're incredibly lucky, you will eventually experience late-paying clients that become non-paying clients. Businesses go under, disputes arise and occasionally a client may just prefer to keep the money! So one day you may need to take steps to recover money owed to you.

First, speak to your client – are they withholding payment for a reason? Are they unhappy with your work, or your invoice? There's probably a good reason why they aren't paying you – such as a lack of funds. You can choose to negotiate with your client, perhaps accepting a percentage of the debt up front with the balance paid at an agreed date. You may be able to agree to spread the payments over a few months, accepting a number of small payments to gradually clear the debt. Finding a solution that suits you both can help you avoid legal proceedings. Make sure you address any outstanding invoice queries, because you can't escalate the case through the courts unless the invoice is undisputed.

Threaten to charge interest

You are legally entitled to charge interest on unpaid debts, at the (current) rate of 8 per cent above the Bank of England base rate. Charging interest can be a good way to motivate your client to pay you faster, but if they just don't have enough money to pay you then adding interest charges to the amount owed won't help either of you.

Send in the solicitors

If your client won't communicate, or you haven't been able to reach an agreement, your next step is likely to be a solicitor's letter. These need not be very expensive – in fact the Thomas Higgins Partnership offers a standard debt recovery letter service for just a few pounds. A solicitor's letter may be enough to motivate your client – it will certainly show them you're deadly serious. If your client still won't pay, then taking them to court may be your only option.

Going to court

There are many debt recovery specialists available who can guide you through the process. The cost of court action is relatively low, and will be mostly paid for by your client. You can either petition the small claims court directly, or use debt recovery specialists to manage the process.

 brilliant recap

- Lack of cash flow could ruin your business – even if you're busy.
- Choose payment terms that favour you.
- Take action at every stage of a project to improve your chances of getting paid promptly.
- Invoice according to your client's conditions.
- Don't be afraid to chase payment.
- If your client won't pay, get the help of a debt recovery specialist – before it's too late.

CHAPTER 22

Create a contract

Contracts are funny things. Contracts can exist without even existing – that is, they can be *implied*. Contracts can also be written or spoken. So, clearly, a contract is more than just a document full of impenetrable language. And yes, you will have a contract with your client even if there is no written contract in place, because the details you agree by email or in person make up the terms of your contract.

In spite of this, there is a benefit to having a formal contract that clearly defines who is doing what, by when and for how much. A written contract can help rein in your client, and can help you recover debts if the job goes awry. Having a contract shows that you're serious. Wielding contracts may scare off timewasters and people who can't really afford you.

Make your own contract

Contracts do not need to be overly complicated. Your contract should simply explain the key details of the project:

- your name and address
- your client's name and address
- project name
- quantity of work involved – number of hours or days on each activity

- due date

- costs

- deliverables – what will the client receive at the end?

- copyright implications – will your client own the copyright immediately, or only once payment is received?

- assumptions – if you're assuming that your client will be providing source material, then specify that in the contract; include any assumptions that you make about your client's responsibilities to contribute to the project.

Sample contract

Freelance web designer, Evie Milo, created a contract template with the help of a lawyer. Evie has generously allowed us to reproduce the contract opposite, but if you would like to use it, I recommend you save yourself the hassle of copying this version and download an electronic copy from Evie's website: **www. eskymo.co.uk** for a small fee.

 brilliant recap

- Contracts exist automatically when you make an agreement with your client.

- The terms of your contract are formed by spoken and written agreements.

- Using a formal contract shows you're serious and may deter time-wasters.

- A formal contract may simplify your case if you have a dispute with your client.

YOUR COMPANY LOGO HERE   **Offer from** COMPANY NAME HERE **to Client**
Dated: Insert the date here

CLIENT CONTACT NAME   YOUR NAME **trading as** COMPANY NAME

CLIENT COMPANY NAME

CLIENT COMPANY ADDRESS   YOUR ADDRESS
CLIENT COMPANY TELEPHONE   YOUR TELEPHONE

('Client')   ('Your Company Name')

Client's Job Reference: JOB NUMBER OR REFERENCE

The Job consists of the following three elements:

1. **Job Outline supplied by Client to** Your Company Name **via insert how the Job was supplied** e.g. by email or telephone or in a meeting **[insert date and time of email / telephone call / meeting]:**

   Outline the brief here – either as you understand it from the conversation you've had with the client or just copy and paste from an email or document supplied. Or you can reference the brief by document name, stating *who* supplied it to you, *how* they supplied it and *when*.

2. **Detailed Job Breakdown proposed by** Your Company **to Client:**

   Project details

   Add a breakdown of the project here. For example:

   Stage 1: Preliminary research
   Stage 2: First draft
   Stage 3: Testing, review or validation
   Stage 4: Final draft

   These stages can then relate to payments – so instead of getting paid one lump sum at the end of a job, you can split the cost down according to stages and get paid as you complete each stage.

   For shorter projects, simply split the payment into two: 50 per cent up front, 50 per cent on completion.

   Required client actions

   • What does the client need to do?
   • What is the client responsible for?
   • What do you need from the client before you can complete the project?
   • List everything that rests with the client because they could easily delay the project (and the deadline you've agreed, simply because they don't do their bit).
   • List all the assumptions that you are making about responsibilities.

▶

3. Agreed Milestone(s), Target Completion Date(s) (TCD) and Fee(s):

No VAT is payable on the Fee and no outlays in respect of the Job are payable unless stated below. Each Proportion of the Total Fee shall be payable upon achievement of the Milestone set next to it, as follows. Upon each Proportion of the Fee being payable, **Your Company** shall issue Client with an invoice in respect of that Proportion and each such invoice *shall be payable by Client upon receipt.*

Milestone(s)	TCD(s)	Proportion of Fee
Stage 1		
'Commencement' if the first payment is due prior to starting the project, otherwise list first stage of project here.	Insert date	£0.00
Proportion of Fee (Stage 1)		**£0.00**
Stage 2		
'Completion' if balance is payable on completion, otherwise include second stage of project here.	Insert date	£0.00
Proportion of Fee (Stage 2)		**£0.00**
Total Fee		**£0.00**

Your Company shall not disclose any of Client's confidential information concerning the Job to any third party without the prior permission of Client.

Please indicate Client's acceptance of this offer, which consists of these **two** pages, by signing, dating and completing the below schedule where indicated:

Authorised Signatory　　**Name of Signatory**　　**Position held by Signatory**
Signing for and on
behalf of Client

....　　...　　...

Date of Signing by Signatory
Signing for and on behalf of Client

....

NB: It's worth including the number of pages on the signature page as that way the client can't claim they didn't receive the entire contract.

PART 6

Next steps –
and beyond!

The rung of a ladder was never meant to rest upon, but only to hold a man's foot long enough to enable him to put the other somewhat higher.
                                                    Thomas Huxley

W hat now then? Have you been following along at home? Have you tried the exercises and followed my advice? Have you been dabbling as a freelancer? I hope you've been having fun and believing me when I say that anyone, with a bit of effort and luck, can become a great freelancer.

The final part of this book is dedicated to the freelancer who wants *more*. If you're still acclimatising to the joys of freelancing then you may wonder how you could possibly want more. Well ... while you can easily freelance for life, many people get a taste for *business* by being freelance, and begin to see bigger possibilities.

Thriving freelancers often encounter a barrier – an impossible hurdle that their freelance status confers: no matter how good you are at selling your services, you only have a fixed amount of time to sell. Rather quickly, you run out of product. Your efforts have an in-built ceiling. And for the enterprising soul on a roll, it's very, very frustrating to run out of product when you've got a buyer. That's why many freelancers find ways to branch out – ways to grow, expand, partner or otherwise overcome the limitations of being the product.

CHAPTER 23

Partnerships, products and businesses

f you want to grow, to take on bigger projects or to diversify your services, then consider teaming up with other freelancers.

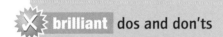 **brilliant** dos and don'ts

When teaming up to power up:

Do

✔ Forge relationships with freelancers you know and trust.

✔ Start small – experiment by working together on small, low-pressure projects.

✔ Define your relationship and responsibilities. Don't make assumptions.

✔ Look for a freelancer with complementary skills. You don't want to work with a carbon-copy of yourself.

Don't

✘ Trust people who haven't earned your trust.

✘ Let a peer piggy-back on your hard work. Make sure your partnership is a genuine partnership and watch out for freeloaders.

✘ Drop everything in favour of the partnership. Attend to your regular clients and your usual sources of income.

✘ Assume that your partner will share your approach to business, your work ethic, or your sense of justice.

Become a business

I know – you're *already* a business. And you are. But what I'm suggesting is that you move from being a micro-business, with you as the sole product, and become a traditional business with a product or a suite of services. There are a few obvious business routes for freelancers:

- become an agency
- package your services as a commodity
- develop your own products.

Let's explore your options.

Become an agency

Seems obvious, right? Clearly, if you're great at finding clients, why not operate as an agency, and farm the work out to freelancers?

A few ideas to get you started as an agency:

- **Choose your partners wisely.** Will you look for an equal partner, or will you hire freelancers to complete elements of the jobs you bring in? Either way, the people you choose can mean the difference between roaring success and miserable failure.

- **Take project management seriously.** Now that other people are completing tasks on your projects, you'll need to manage their time. If you have several different freelancers all working on different, inter-linked elements of a project, then the successful management of those people becomes crucial to your success.

- **Look bigger, act bigger.** Many agencies are little more than a collection of freelancers, so don't hesitate to represent yourself as an agency even if you don't have a fancy office packed with full-timers. In order to land large jobs, you'll need to look like you're ready to handle them. If you want to be an agency, start looking like one.

● **Get together in the same space.** Your projects will flow smoothly if you can collaborate in a shared space. Many coworking spaces and traditional office units offer meeting rooms you can hire by the hour or day. Alternatively, just meet in one of the gazillion coffee shops that exist in every town.

Package your services as products

The trouble with freelancing is that your product is limited. So why not adapt your services into replicable products? Here are a few examples:

● **Writers** – if you are constantly asked to write similar content for similar clients, why not produce a batch of standard documents? Your clients pay less for these documents and you can sell more because you're not writing them from scratch each time. You can also offer a program of updates, so your clients pay a nominal monthly fee in order to receive updated documents twice a year. You could create white-label documents that your clients can then brand as their own.

● **Web designers** – create templates for popular programs like WordPress, Drupal or Joomla. Huge numbers of people are building their own websites, but they want professional, flexible designs, so cater to this market. Once your templates are built, you can sell infinite copies.

● **Everyone else** – why not package your knowledge into ebooks? With the right marketing, you could earn a recurring income from your accumulated wisdom. Write it once, sell it a thousand times.

Another promising route is to adapt your services into a support package. So if your clients are likely to need your help once or twice a year, offer them a support contract or an agreement so they can pay a monthly fee to spread the cost of your services. By getting monthly direct debit payments flowing into your bank, you'll have a regular, predictable income that will help you grow as a business.

For any freelancer planning to shift away from being a technician for hire, I recommend *The E-Myth Revisited*, by Michael E. Gerber (HarperCollins, 1994). The 'e' stands for entrepreneur, and the book deals with common misconceptions about business, and common problems that trouble young businesses. The central problem is that many technicians – people like you – think they can take their skill and turn it into a business. But what those technicians don't realise is that a business is much more than just a skill. A business needs systems, a clear vision, and a consistent delivery of that vision in order to survive. As you bring people on board, it's essential that every person working for your business has the same clear vision of your purpose, and that every customer you serve gets a consistent experience. So start thinking about what the vision of your business really is, and how you can communicate this with your colleagues.

> a business is much more than just a skill

 brilliant recap

● Form partnerships with freelancers you trust.

● Escalate from freelancer to agency – just start acting like one.

● Package your services as replicable products to increase your capacity to sell.

● Becoming a bigger business does require different thinking – so think carefully before leaping into something new.

Looking forward

Freelance forever

 'Don't die wondering'.

Anon

Don't let this talk of creating products and starting businesses diminish your delight about being freelance; there is no need to stop what you're doing. You can remain freelance for all your days, if that makes you happy. You can do whatever you like – there's no *right* way. You can go back to regular employment. You can grow a beard, eat cheese and listen to folk music. You can continue to develop your skills and hone your services – and you can be happy doing it.

Bigger is not always better

Freelancing has a habit of supercharging your inner passions – spurring you on to all kinds of achievements – but growth and development can all be enjoyed as a freelancer, so if you're happy as you are, don't feel compelled to change. Your freelance licence will not expire.

And freelancers, just like cheese, improve with age.

The benefits of being an experienced freelancer

- You have more experience than everyone.

- You're better at quoting, proposing, presenting, pitching and, well, *everything* than every other freelancer in your area.

- You have enough contacts, sending you enough referrals to keep you busy until Mars becomes habitable.

But sadly, it's not all fluffy kittens and unending delights ...

The hazards of being an experienced freelancer (and how to avoid them)

- Your age and wisdom are seen as limitations. Avoid becoming a victim of age-discrimination. Don't act like a teenager, but instead trade on your experience. Accept a role as the seasoned campaigner, and act it with pride.

- Your skills become out-dated. Easy to avoid, this one – just don't settle into a routine or rely on ageing technologies or formats. Don't cling to sinking ships. Be prepared to retrain, to adapt and to start new things. You might be getting older, but you don't have to roll over and die.

- All your clients and contacts retire. Being a brilliant freelancer does introduce you to the danger of *peaking*. Your clients get bigger and better, your day rate swells, every aspect of your operation becomes smoother until jobs are virtually completing themselves. But you reach a pinnacle, and start dropping down the other side. You've explored all your connections, maximised the potential of every opportunity and hit a dead end. Decline ensues. To avoid this scenario, simply keep on pushing on. Be relentless in your efforts. Don't become complacent. Your current successes are owed to hard work and persistent effort.

Continued success requires more hard work and persistent, relentless effort. You can't stop pushing because you've reached the summit.

Kick-start a flagging freelance career

Ashka is a freelance designer. She's been working hard for six months, and although she's funded her life solely on her freelance career, her earnings are more beans and rice than caviar and Ferrero Rocher. Ashka loves the freedoms and challenges that freelancing brings her, but she fears she will never earn enough money to make it profitable.

If Ashka was a real person, and not a construct to illustrate my point, I would ask her these two questions:

'How well are you marketing yourself?'

Marketing is all about creating *opportunities* for work. You need opportunities. Lots of them. Great big bags of opportunities, dripping with possibilities. How many paths lead people to you? Do you have a good spread of marketing channels, with work coming from your website, social networks, real world networks, phone calls, direct mail or emails? Have you left any big marketing channels untapped? If you're struggling to get good levels of work, but you've never tried networking, then

> how many paths lead people to you?

it's likely that you're struggling because you're invisible. Get out there. If you're struggling but you haven't got a website, then it's likely that you're struggling because your competitors have a significant advantage. There are plenty of freelancers who thrive without one or other of these things, but they thrive in *spite* of that, not because of it. If you're struggling, you need to look for work everywhere.

'Are you trading off your successes?'

Being a freelancer is like many things in life: the route to the top consists of many steps. To reach the top, you have to start stepping. You can't leap to the top without taking every step in between, and so it is with freelancing. You can't dive into freelancing, scoop up all the best clients, do all the best work and rake in the cash. Oh no! You have to start

___
you have to start small
___

small. Bigger clients typically hire freelancers who work with bigger clients. So the challenge is to work with a bigger client before you've worked with a bigger client. Are you scratching your head yet? Sorry – I'm referring to the age-old conundrum of jobs that require experienced practitioners. How does anyone get experience in the first place?

The determined freelancer *will* get the experience – that part is not so hard. The real skill is in using one experience to catapult you on to the next big job. I like to view freelancing as a game of stepping stones. You can hop gradually from one success to another, but to do that you must publicise your achievements. So if you have a website, a social media presence or a LinkedIn profile, make sure you update them with your latest achievements. The world is not watching your every move, and the world is not talking about you, so if you want anyone to know about your successes, you must tell them. Be your own cheerleader. And cheer loudly.

Tomorrow starts today

 'There is no chance, no destiny, no fate, that can hinder or control the firm resolve of a determined soul.'

Ella Wheeler Wilcox

Before we go, I want to reflect on the qualities that are invaluable to the aspiring freelancer. Beyond all else, I reckon *stubbornness* is key. Freelance careers rarely take off without a persistent push. From start to finish, you'll encounter lots of small catastrophes – and after every tumble you'll need to haul yourself up and launch forward with more energy and purpose than before.

- Be relentless in all things.
- Never give up on quality, because the quality of your work is what you're selling. Your marketing will count for nought if your product is substandard.
- Meet people. Making friends and expanding your horizons are one of the joys of freelancing.
- Act like a business because you *are* a business.
- Marketing is your foundation. Keep on marketing, even when you're busy. Try new things. See what works. Drop the things that don't help and do more of what works.

In closing this book, I would like to repeat my thanks to all the people who helped make it happen. Beyond the contributors, there are many generous people who shared their hard-learned wisdom with me, encouraged me, and listened to my concerns when things were tough. And to you, the reader, thanks for trusting this book to guide your freelance adventure. I hope you've found it useful. Whether you freelance for life, or just a few happy months, good luck.

For more freelance advice go to: **www.brilliantfreelancer.com**

Index

the
brilliant series

9780273742524 — brilliant Business Plan — What to know and do to make the perfect plan

9780273742555 — brilliant Email — How to win back time and increase your productivity

9780273740544 — brilliant Influence — What the most influential people know, do and say

9780273743231 — brilliant Manager — What the best managers know, do and say

9780273735373 — brilliant Accounting — Everything you need to know to manage the success of your accounts

9780273743248 — brilliant Negotiations — What the best negotiators know, do and say

9780273737452 — brilliant Online Marketing — How to use the internet to market your business

9780273744092 — brilliant Time Management — What the most productive people know, do and say

9780273744580 — brilliant Business Writing — How to inspire, engage and persuade through words

9780273722328 — brilliant Project Management — What the best project managers know, do and say

9780273720591 — brilliant Leader — What the best leaders know, do and say

9780273726463 — brilliant Selling — What the best salespeople know, do and say

9780273725114 — brilliant Pitch — What to know, do and say to make the perfect pitch

9780273717355 — brilliant Coaching — How to be a brilliant coach in your workplace

9780273743217 — brilliant Networking — What the best networkers know, do and say

9780273721239 — brilliant Marketing — What the best marketers know, do and say

9780273730675 — brilliant Presentation — What the best presenters know, do and say

9780273727347 — brilliant Copywriting — How to craft the most interesting and effective copy imaginable

9780273721826 — brilliant Meetings — What to know, do and say to have fewer, better meetings

9780273738077 — brilliant Customer Service — What to know, do and say to keep your customers happy

**Whatever your level, we'll get you to the next one.
It's all about you. Get ready to shine!**